Printed in USA by Rizzo & Associates LLC, www.rizzoandassociates.com

ISBN 978-0-692-87901-6

Contents

A Work-on-You Book

This book is dedicated to all women, everywhere. It is for you regardless of your age, ethnicity, race, identity, parental or marital status, ability, or economic status. Although I have met hundreds of thousands of women in my personal and professional life, I have never met one that couldn't accomplish what she wanted to do, if she set her mind to it. This book is in tribute to you. It is my best hope that this *work-on-you* book will assist you in becoming all you were meant to be.

At first glance, this may look like a workbook, but it isn't. It is a *work-on-you* book. You don't have to be sick to get better, and the purpose of this book is to help you become a better, stronger, greater you. In each chapter you will have several opportunities to take a close look at yourself, your thoughts, feelings, habits, lifestyle and relationships. Get a notebook so you can record your answers to each of the self-exploration and planning activities that appear in each chapter. By the time you finish this e-book you will have written your own book to guide you through your life. Consider it your self-therapy journal and look at it whenever you need to feel strong and confident.

To encourage an open dialog, and thus assure that you receive optimum benefit from the book, I have launched a Facebook group where you can reach me anytime at www.facebook.com/groups/greaterwomaninalesserworld/. I encourage you to challenge the ideas you are about to ingest. I invite you to join with me and the women who read this book and really dig into the issues it raises. You can also contact me at ritar@rizzoandassociates.com or through our website at www.rizzoandassociates.com .

Let's dialog, discuss and debate. Let's laugh and cry and giggle and throw our hands in the air in celebration of ourselves and one another. Let's form a mastermind alliance that brings the best out in all of us. Let's author my next book by bringing together our collective wisdom and experience in unstoppable synergy. Let's form the Sisterhood of the Golden Goddess.

 Meet the Golden Goddess. She lives within you and is ever present in this book. She will challenge you to take a hard look at your soft spots, to clarify your beliefs, to test your values, and to take positive action on your own behalf. At times you may feel confused or conflicted by what the Goddess is asking of you. The Goddess' guidance will sometimes create a great insight for you that you are bursting to share with others. These are the times you will want to post on the Facebook group. To access the Facebook group simply join or login to Facebook and type the words "Greater Woman in a Lesser World" into the search box. The group will come up and give you the option to join. Thereafter it will be listed in your "groups" list on your homepage.

Hopefully, you are reading this book, and participating in the activities herein to create a better life for yourself and those you hold dear, and to make a greater contribution to the world around you. It is my fondest wish that you find, in these pages, the guidance that will awaken your inner Goddess, and put you on the path to achieve the fullest degree of greatness possible.

Let's talk soon!

Rita

Your Purpose in the Lesser World

"The best way to make the world a better place is to make you a better person." Lou Vincent

Joblessness, recession, foreclosures, sky-rocketing credit card interest, wars, political strife, protests, poverty....and the list goes on. As Grandmaster Flash the rapper said, "Don't push me 'cause I'm close to the edge. I'm trying not to lose my head. It's like a jungle sometimes. It makes me wonder how I keep from going under!"

Raise your hand if you think the world needs to be a better place. Oh look, everyone raised their hand. The world fails to live up to our hopes, dreams and expectations daily. As women we are fearful...afraid of the future our children face in a world where opportunities are shrinking and problems are growing. We fear for our parents whose golden years may not glow all that brightly given their fixed income and failing health. We fear for our significant others whose dreams fade more with each passing year as the realities of today's world bear down upon them. Oh yes, and we fear for ourselves...our health...our sanity.

Typical, huh? We fear for ourselves last! Daily we hear our female friends lament about how someone else in their life is suffering, and how they are trying to take care of the situation. Then they tell us about how they are neglecting themselves. Neglecting themselves? Most women take little, if any, care of themselves. They forget to take their vitamins, won't rest an injury, skip the gym, cover anxiety with a glass of wine, spend sleepless nights wracked with worry, deprive themselves of new shoes and foot comfort because the kids need shoes worse, and generally martyr themselves for the cause of others.

In a nutshell, that is what this book is really about. If you are consistently sick, exhausted, overwhelmed, under-motivated, depressed, despondent, unfulfilled, or just plain pissed, you are not taking care of yourself. If you are unwell, you cannot give your all to those in the world that you care most about. This, of course, has a ripple effect. Those who depend on your loved ones suffer in kind. Thusly, your misery spirals out into the world, and the world becomes a lesser place based on your contribution to it. The outcomes of self-neglect are pretty devastating. So much so, that they actually make a universal impact over time.

My husband, the wise man who spouted the quote at the top of the page, is full of witty and wise one-liners. My personal favorite is "If Mama ain't happy, nobody's happy!" True that! Just insert one miserable woman into a room full of people, and soon everyone will feel mournful. The Emotional IQ of the room devolves to that possessed by the most emotionally upset person present.

It is my belief that humans are sent to earth to serve one another in a manner that honors their creator. To live a life of servitude is something that most women are used to. We serve our children, our parents, our mates, our friends and our extended family members. We serve society in a myriad of ways, by being kind to strangers, through volunteerism, and even by being slaves to the latest fashion trends so that we are aesthetically pleasing to all who pass by. We are great at serving others and expect that they will care for us in kind. And when they don't mama ain't happy!

Truth be told, most of us deserved to be better served by others. Those we serve might take us for granted, and sometimes try to use us until they use us up! So we get tired, and irritable, and sometimes even become chronically unhappy. And that is not the saddest truth. The saddest truth is that we do much to contribute to our own unhappiness by putting our own needs last and acting as though it is someone else's job to make us happy. Each of us must do that for ourselves. It is time to grant yourself a promotion from last to first on your list of people to serve. By being good to yourself you will not only become happier, but you will be able to provide even better service to others as well.

In order to be healthy and happy, a woman must attend to her mind, body and soul. Furthermore, each element of a holistically healthy life must be in balance. It is only then that a woman can experience true and consistent happiness, and fulfill her purpose in life. That's a pretty big statement, isn't it? Think about it for a moment. Do you know a woman who prays almost non-stop but is out of shape and full of aches and pains? Her spiritual life may be intact, but her daily life is not much easier because of it. Ever meet a woman who is in good shape physically but lives in a constant state of worry? The mind rules the body, not the converse! She is still in significant danger of becoming ill. In short, if you want to make the world a better place, you must begin where you have the most control. You must begin with you.

Caring for yourself holistically will not only result in increased health and improved happiness, it will cause you to learn and grow rapidly. It will serve as your launch pad to greatness.

Greatness

It is never too late for you to be great. Aspiring to greatness is a worthy goal, and one that many women never consider. It is much more common for men to want to be great, than for woman. Even in these enlightened times, women are not encouraged to do great things and change the world in sweeping strokes.

About a decade ago I was having dinner with a woman I had met earlier in the day. She was a beautiful, energetic, intelligent young woman who was telling me that she planned to move to a large city. She felt she would have more opportunity there. "What sort of opportunity are you looking for?" I queried. Before answering she leaned across the table and lowered her voice to a whisper. "Ever since I was a little girl I have known I was destined for greatness," she revealed softly. "I am looking for an opportunity to do great things." I responded by telling her that I too, had always harbored the feeling that I was born to do great things, but had never spoken about it to anyone. Why were we whispering? Why would it have been so embarrassing for the strangers around us to know that we wanted to do great things? Men speak loudly about their pursuit of greatness. Isn't it time women did the same?

Do you aspire to greatness? Do you want to do phenomenal things that will change the world in significant and sweeping ways? You can you know. Simply by becoming holistically healthy you will accomplish more in your immediate sphere of influence. But why stop there? Start by becoming a greater woman than you are right now. Finish by becoming the woman you were always meant to be, one that astonishes the world. It is possible. It is within your grasp. You can make the lesser world into something more. Let's get started.

The first step involves defining who you are, where you are, and where you want to go. Do you believe that each of us has a purpose? I can see you nodding in the affirmative. Strangely, most people believe that everyone has a purpose, but when asked to state their own purpose, they can seldom do so. Do you know what your purpose is? If not, let's find out!

Tune up Your Brain

You are about to take a trip down memory lane. In order to discover your true purpose, the purpose you were born to fulfill, you will need to recall your earliest childhood memories. For some this will be a relatively easy task, but for others it is difficult. You may have blocked out large chunks of your childhood memories, especially if childhood was a painful period of your life. This doesn't mean those memories are gone, but they may be hard for you to access.

Neurological studies suggest that memory is best triggered by scents and sounds; specifically musical or rhythmic sounds. If you find it difficult to access the memories that you are asked to recall to identify your purpose, first listen to some of the music specific to each period of your life, or sing a song that you recall from each period. You can also recite nursery rhymes that you learned or were read to you as a child. Additionally you can sniff a scent from each life period. The scents of flowers, trees, cleaning products, perfumes and fresh fruits can take you back to an earlier time. It won't be long before a scene unfolds before you with you as its centerpiece. In this way you can re-experience your childhood, teen and early adult years.

Focus on the activities and experiences that you most enjoyed, the gifts you possessed, and the skills you have mastered without much effort during each period in your early life.

Your Unique Purpose

Sit back and relax. Close your eyes. Think about yourself as a small girl. Ponder these questions for as long as necessary, then open your eyes and jot down your thoughts in the box below.

When you were a little girl...

What games and toys did you love?
What kinds of fantasies did you enjoy acting out?
What were the most fun activities for you?
What were you really good at?
What role did you take in your group of friends?
What subjects in school did you enjoy the most?

Now think about your teen years. Open your eyes and make note of your thoughts.

When you were a teen...

What organizations did you join?
What leadership roles did you assume?
What did others think you would most likely achieve?
When you were the happiest?
What were your best assets?
What traits did you admire in others?
One final focus. Now think of yourself as a young woman. Remember your college days or your first job, or both. You know the drill...write it down.

When you were a young woman...

What tasks did you excel in doing?
What kind of people were you drawn to?
What were some points of pride for you?
What was the most important lesson you learned?
What made you feel happy and excited?
What inspired you to work hard?

Your life's purpose was determined before you took your first breath. It has been revealing itself to you since. Review what you just finished writing. Do you see a pattern? Is there a theme to your life that you may have failed to notice up to now? Your purpose in life is supported by your talents, your interests, your character and your personality. Study the three boxes until you see the consistencies, and then write 3-5 sentences in the box below. This statement will succinctly state your life purpose.

My Life Purpose is...

Congratulations! You have made your first step in better knowing and understanding the greater woman that lives within you. Furthermore, you have made a liberating move towards fulfilling your life's purpose by identifying it. Perhaps up to this point you have allowed others to define you. In an attempt to please others in your life you have engaged in many activities that don't interest or inspire you. You have put your own needs aside to meet the needs of others. You can now limit that activity, or stop it completely, and focus on fulfilling your purpose.

I was relatively lucky. Someone shared this exercise with me when I was in my late 20's. I discovered at that time that my purpose was to *use my quick mind to learn as much as possible, convert my knowledge into lessons that would be useful to others, and to share my lessons in a manner that enriches those I encounter.* When I came to this insight I immediately began setting limits on how I invested my time. My purpose had nothing to do with keeping food fresh, so I stopped going to dreaded Tupperware parties. When I was in charge of an event such as a baby shower, I designed the activities to be in concert with my purpose. Instead of playing party games I asked the guests to video a special message or piece of advice to the expectant mother. Not only did it feel good to be authentic and true to myself, but others were quick to compliment my unique approaches. It is no surprise that when you consistently do what you are best at your results are stellar!

How will your life change now that you have clearly identified your purpose? What will you limit? What will you pursue? Take a moment and jot down your thoughts. What will you do more of, less of, and the same amount of, to be true to your purpose?

From this day forward, I will do...
More
Less
Same

How are you feeling right now? Focused? Strong? Empowered? The first step in your journey to holistic health and ultimate greatness is truly an uplifting one! Read your purpose statement and the more, less, same box each day until you have committed them to memory. Remember, s/he who defines you controls you. Doesn't it feel exhilarating to be in full control of yourself?

A Real Woman

Josey was floundering. She felt unfulfilled and like she was always running but never getting anywhere. She had recently come to the realization that her life was not her own. She was contorting herself into who others expected her to be. At age 40 she yearned to finally become her own person. While attending a workshop on mission and goal setting for her job she began to consider using the same process to discover her personal life mission.

After conducting a life review similar to the activity you just completed, Josey discovered that her purpose in life was to be a calligrapher. Although she didn't quit her job as a clerical assistant she did start advertising on Craigslist to make hand printed wedding invitations and party favors using calligraphy. Soon she had enough orders to fund her own website. After two years of dedicating most of her spare time to her business she was able to quit her job and begin doing what she loved on a fulltime basis.

"Just making a success of my own business has changed my life," Josey admitted during a recent interview. "I now feel confident and right," she stated. "I was always full of doubt, never knowing if I was making the best decisions in my life. Now I am sure of myself. I am better at setting limits on the demands others place on me, and I spend the majority of my time doing what I want to do rather than what I feel I have to do. I think I finally know who I am, and I enjoy that person a great deal."

Mind Your Mind

"The mind is everything. What you think you become." Buddha

Buddha is right, you know. You do become whatever you think about most of the time. If you see yourself as a successful, confident person of integrity, you become one. On the other hand, if you see yourself as a person with low self-esteem, who may fail at any moment...well, that's who you are!

On my first business trip to London a number of years ago I was fascinated by the signage I saw throughout the city. Many signs began with the word "mind." Mind the oncoming traffic, mind the roving gangs of thugs, mind the gap (no, it didn't mean sit with your knees together as I suspected, it meant don't fall into the gap between the subway platform and the train!) Obviously the British are big fans of using one's mind to insure one's safety.

Interesting thought isn't it? Use your mind to protect yourself. It encourages you to pay attention. In the case of the signage in London, it means you must pay attention to your environment. Although this is sound advice, a greater danger exists. Many of us pay no attention to our own thoughts. We don't realize that the critic within is a far more potent and constant enemy than any "roving band of thugs" who may accost us. We will come back to the thug problem when we talk about the body in the next chapter, but for now let's focus on the way we think about ourselves.

"Oh no," you may be thinking. Now we are going to talk about positive mental attitude. Well, yes and no. We are going to talk about your self-image, how you see yourself and how you integrate feedback from others about who you are. Too many women allow others to shape their self-image. This is a real contradiction. SELF-image should be formed by your own view of yourself, not based on how others see you.

Self-image finds its roots in self-esteem. Self-esteem can be defined as the degree to which you value yourself. Is self-esteem earned or given? The correct answer is both. When you were a child, the way others regarded you formed the foundation of your self-esteem. If your friends, family and teachers held you in high regard, you learned that you were valuable, significant and important, and you acted in ways that supported that belief. Unfortunately most adults aren't fortunate enough to have escaped some form of cruelty in childhood.

You may have formed some very unflattering ideas about yourself from your peers, teachers, parents, siblings and early experiences. Regrettable as that is, it isn't pertinent to your life today. As adults, self-esteem is earned. When you take an action that induces guilt, regret, embarrassment or pain, you lower your value in your own eyes. This might bring to mind the negative messages you integrated about yourself as a child, but your early mindset isn't the problem, your current behavior is.

If you change your mind about who you are, you will also change the way you behave. If you behave better because you think more of yourself, it becomes a self-perpetuating cycle. The more good things you do, the better you feel about yourself, and the more your self-esteem rises. Much like self-image, self-confidence is also rooted in self-esteem. The more frequently you get successful results from your endeavors, the more your confidence grows. Gaining confidence in yourself can lead to taking amazing risks, accepting huge challenges, and ultimately becoming a highly successful person. You can overcome shaky self-esteem in two ways, think differently about yourself, and behave differently than you ever have before.

Since it is a human tendency to be mindlessly guided by our past perceptions of ourselves, I would like to invite you to take a self-assessment that will help you discover the exact nature of your current thinking and behavior. Once you have taken the assessment you can decide on what you would like to improve, and you will notice the strengths that form the foundation of your character.

Characteristics of High and Low Self-esteem

In Column A, on a scale of 1-10, place the number where you were on each characteristic 5 years ago. In Column B place the number where you are now. In Column C place an X in the 4 areas where you would most like to improve. (Example: If you often felt like a victim 5 years ago, you would rate the first item on this chart a 10 in Column A. In Column B you might rate this item as a 5 if you believe that you have improved significantly over the past 5 years and now only think of yourself as a victim about half as often as you used to. If you would like to consciously work on improving this area more in the future put an X in Column C.)

Characteristics of Low Self-esteem	A	B	C
1. I feel and act like a victim.			
2. I am judgmental of myself and others.			
3. I break agreements and violate my own standards.			
4. I am covert and phony.			
5. I am self-deprecating, shame-filled and blaming.			
6. I am critical and condemning of myself and others.			
7. I am a "nice" person, approval seeking, a people pleaser			
8. I have a negative attitude.			
9. I rationalize frequently.			
10. I am jealous and envious of others.			
11. I am a perfectionist.			
12. I have dependencies, addictions and/or self-destructive behavior			
13. I am complacent and/or stagnant.			
14. I don't like to work with others.			
15. I fail to complete tasks regularly.			
16. I judge my self-worth by comparing myself to others. I feel inferior.			
17. I don't accept or give compliments often or well.			
18. I worry excessively.			
19. I am fearful of exploring my "real self."			
20. I shun new endeavors because I fear mistakes or failures.			
21. I am run by my emotions or have irrational emotions.			
22. I lack purpose in my life.			
23. I am inadequate to handle emergency situations.			
24. When I lose at something I feel resentful or inferior.			
25. I am vulnerable to other's opinions, comments and attitudes.			

(Example: Look at the first item. If you feel you took appropriate risks about half as often as you needed to 5 years ago you would put a 5 in Column A. If you currently take appropriate risks on a consistent basis you would place a 10 in Column B. If you are satisfied with your current level of risk-taking you would not mark Column C.)

Characteristics of High Self-esteem	A	B	C
1. I take appropriate risks.			
2. I take responsibility for my life and the consequences of my actions.			
3. My life has purpose, is goal directed, and committed.			
4. I am honest with myself and others emotionally and intellectually.			
5. I face my fears and move through them.			
6. I admit mistakes, and accept the limitations of my abilities.			
7. I own my strengths and respect, nourish, accept and love myself.			
8. I do my own thinking and make my own decisions.			
9. I extend forgiveness to myself and others.			
10. I have a high degree of tenacity and persistence.			
11. I have an attitude of gratitude.			
12. I am accepting of myself and others.			
13. I set internal standards, principles and values and live by them.			
14. I see opportunities instead of problems.			
15. I am enthusiastic, spontaneous and have a zest for living.			
16. I praise myself and others genuinely and without reserve.			
17. I have the courage of my convictions.			
18. I seek continual growth. I am a lifelong learner.			
19. I can appropriately ask for help when I need it.			
20. I anticipate new endeavors with quiet confidence.			
21. I enjoy being by myself occasionally.			
22. I actively participate in life.			
23. I share my real self with others.			
24. I go for excellence, but not perfectionism.			
25. Allow myself to be human.			

It is time to analyze your chart. For now, just consider the items you marked in Column C. These are areas you have chosen for improvement. Later you may want to review these charts and mark other items for improvement, but for at present please focus on the areas you have already targeted.

Now that you have completed your low and high self-esteem assessments just sit quietly for a few moments and consider your results. How do they make you feel? What are you thinking as you notice your current traits and the progress or regression you have experienced over the past five years. After you have allowed your results to soak in continue on to the next page where you will be asked to develop a short plan as to how to become a more self-esteeming woman.

Choose five items from the low self-esteem assessment that you wish to improve upon. These should be items that make you feel sad, guilty, gutless, ashamed or uneasy. List the items in order of priority from most to least bothersome in the box below. If you have more than five you can always come back and replace the current items on your list where you have successfully vanquished the impulse to react to them negatively, and replace them with new items to work on.

Priority Order	Low Esteem Characteristics Selected

The items you just listed can be addressed by making a conscious effort to catch yourself in the act, and interrupting the behavior or thinking that you are experiencing. When you find yourself acting in these low-esteeming ways replace your current thinking and behavior with what you believe to be the opposite reaction. For example, if you feel and act like a victim, the next time you are doing so, stop what you are doing by saying to yourself, "I am not a victim. My choices have led me to the place I am in. I will take responsibility for getting myself out of the situation I am facing and will not wait for others to rescue me."

Now focus on the assessment that lists the high self-esteem characteristics. In the table below record the top five strengths you currently possess that will assist you in overcoming the low self-esteem items that you wish to rid yourself of. Focus on high scores in Column B to find your strongest self-esteeming characteristics.

Priority Order	High Esteem Characteristics Selected

The high-esteeming items you just listed are affirmations. Please memorize them. Any time you are tempted to succumb to your low self-esteem characteristics you are to immediately repeat the five high self-esteem traits to yourself either mentally or by speaking them aloud, or both. You may need to repeat them several times before you feel the strength that they can provide you. You will know that you have repeated them an adequate number of times when you actually feel like the person that you are telling yourself that you are. By that time the impulse to think or behave negatively will have passed and you will find it easy to resist the temptation to engage in the negative behavior that makes you feel bad about yourself.

I know. You may be thinking that this is too easy, that it simply won't work for you. You are wrong about that. The only way you will know for sure if this works or not is to try it. Just do this for a week, and then review your progress. Do you feel better? Are you less worried? Have you said or done fewer things that you regret moments after perpetrating the behavior? If so, continue on using this technique for a second week. It generally takes about eight weeks of mindful focus on your strengths to diminish your weaknesses.
But what if no one else notices the changes that you have made? So what? It matters little if others see you evolving towards the bigger, better person you have chosen to become. You will have noticed, and you are the person you must impress. You cannot escape yourself no matter how hard you try, and you can be a happier, healthier person without notice or permission from anyone else.

Perhaps you are thinking that I just don't appreciate how difficult the others in your life are, and how they can pull you away from even your best intentions. Again, it matters little if you are residing in a maximum security women's prison or in a grass hut on a Hawaiian beach. Only you can form your thoughts. Only you can modify your feelings. Only you can act with integrity, even when it is absent from those around you.

The messages you send yourself about who you are shape your life. You attract to yourself what you think about the most. Once you begin to focus on your strengths you will simultaneously starve your weaknesses. The mind cannot entertain two thoughts at the same time. Try thinking of two things at once. You can't do it, can you? You can think one thing, and then sneak another thought in real fast behind it, but even the best multi-taskers can only focus on one thought at a time. Don't fall into the trap of thinking about your affirmation, then follow it with a "Yes, but..." If tempted to do so, repeat the affirmation or move quickly to another one.

Your thoughts shape your emotions. If you have ever said to another person, "You make me mad!" or "You hurt my feelings," or "You make me happy," you are misstating what is actually happening. You generate a feeling after you have done a brief appraisal of the situation at hand. I know that it often seems that you feel first and then think afterwards, but that is a physiological impossibility. Even when you are startled and instantly fearful your brain has registered a thought that caused you to feel fearful. "What was that?" "Who's there?" "This plane is going down!" registers in your brain before you are gripped by fear.

Thoughts ➔ Emotions ➔ Reactions ➔ Behavior

If you want to change your behavior you must start with your thinking. On the off chance that you cannot change your thoughts in time and a negative emotion occurs, you have another chance to interrupt the process before you manifest a negative reaction. You can choose different thoughts which will alter the ensuing emotional state. If you are unable to vanquish the negative emotion you can use your thoughts again to decide upon your reaction. "I feel angry but instead of showing that emotion I will laugh it off." "I want to cry but instead I will leave the room." "I have an urge to tell you off but I will ask you questions in a kind tone instead."

The key to reprogramming yourself is to practice...practice...practice! Be aware of your thinking. Change it whenever it isn't serving you well. Mind your mind and soon you will have greater control over your life.

A Real Woman

Susan was just like her mother. Everyone said so. She was miserable. Maybe it was because she had been taught to be worried and negative, a person who had low trust for others and no trust for herself. She found herself gossiping about one friend to another, criticizing the smallest of flaws in others. At every family gathering she moved from one person to another bemoaning her life and seeking reassurance that it was not her fault that she was in whatever predicament she had found herself in at the moment. Quick to anger and slow to forgive, Susan knew she was unpleasant to be around and she realized that others avoided her because she was indeed, just like her mother.

After carefully assessing her level of self-esteem Susan made a plan to improve her attitude. She developed a sense of gratitude that she had never experienced before. Several times daily she took the time to count her blessings and give thanks for the small things that were going right in her life. She stopped being phony and covert by making a rule for herself that required her to talk to people about their faults instead of talking about them to others. She soon discovered that most of the time the flaws she criticized in a gossipy manner didn't seem important enough to address directly, and she let go of the perceived slights without confrontation.

Susan began to cultivate a zest for life and now makes it a point to greet each day with enthusiasm instead of dread. Sure, she still made mistakes, but she quit endlessly kicking her own butt for making them. She allowed herself the gift of her own forgiveness, and also began to forgive others when they fell short of her expectations. Even her mother has noticed the positive change in her and they are better able to enjoy each other now.

Curiosity

"The desire to know is natural to good men." Leonardo da Vinci

One sure way to expand your mind and advance your thinking is to be curious. Remember when you were child who was curious about everything? Did you retain that trait or do you now feel that you are better off if you don't discover anything new? If you are not ever vigilant, life will beat you down. The older you get, the less curious you will become. By the time you are age 30 you have received enough negative messages and experiences that you begin to rein in your curiosity, and the exuberant feelings derived from discovering something new. The more you suppress the urge to be curious, the less natural curiosity you will allow to manifest in your life.

The old saying, "Curiosity killed the cat, but satisfaction brought it back," has a rather negative connotation. It is something we say to children to get them to stop poking around in affairs that should not concern them. Your initial programming with regard to curiosity may not have been designed to promote this highly valuable human trait. Curiosity is also negatively associated with nosiness, gossip, and even clumsiness. "Watch where you are going!" "Mind your own business!" "Don't stare at them!" "What are you looking at?" All of these directives are curiosity killers.

When curiosity dies the desire to learn and grow vanishes with it. Curiosity nourishes both the mind and the soul. It causes your thinking to expand. It excites your imagination. It teaches you something. It makes you feel more alive. It breeds initiative and action.

A few years ago I had a young woman in one of my classes who had a hard time staying awake. Even at break she failed to perk up. At lunch I approached her when the two of us were alone in the room. "Doesn't today's topic interest you?" I asked. "Nothing interests me," she replied. "I hate stuff that makes me think."

At first I thought she was depressed, but as the afternoon progressed I noticed that she was quite attentive to her cellphone and had no problem being engaged by the social media posts from her friends. She simply had no curiosity about new learning. Learning moves a person out of their comfort zone and forces them to explore new ideas and concepts that may not be congruent with their current system of beliefs. Learning involves effort and it isn't always fun, but it is necessary in order for your mind and soul to evolve.

Advice from da Vinci

In his book *How to Think Like Leonardo da Vinci* (1998) by Michael J. Gelb, Mr. Geib outlines seven steps to every day genius. The seven principles that da Vinci used to become a timeless genius include curiosity, demonstration, sensitization, embracing uncertainty, art and science, cultivation of grace, ambidexterity, fitness and poise, and the appreciation of the connection of all things. I would encourage you to buy the book and work through all of the principles, but for the purpose of our discussion we will concentrate on the first principle, that of curiosity.

Have you noticed how each generation is smarter that the one who came before them? Today's infants seem to reach their developmental milestones observably faster than their parents did. Simply in order to keep up with these Baby Einsteins, we must shorten our learning curve, and develop our minds to the fullest extent possible. Freud said of da Vinci, "He transmuted his passion into inquisitiveness." Let's engage in a few of the strategies used by da Vinci to foster the genius in ourselves that we need to adequately face the challenges that we find ourselves facing in the lesser world in which we live, whether it be keeping up with our children and grandchildren, or simply navigating daily life. Curiosity is the mother of creativity and who among us doesn't wish to be more creative in finding ways to cope with kids, extended family, friends, work challenges and societal issues.

How Curious are You?

To begin, please take Gelb's Curiosity Self-assessment to discover your current level of curiosity. Please check all of the habits that you currently use to spur on your curiosity.

✓   **Curiosity Factors**

I keep a journal to record my insights and questions.
I take adequate time for contemplation and reflection.
I am always learning something new.
When faced with an important decision, I actively seek out different perspectives.
I am a voracious reader.
I learn from little children.
I am skilled at identifying and solving problems.
My friends would describe me as open-minded and curious.
When I hear or read a new word or phrase, I look it up and make note of it.
I know a lot about other cultures and am always learning more.
I know or am involved in learning a new language.
I solicit feedback from friends, relatives and colleagues.
I love learning.

How did you do? All thirteen items are essential to refresh your sense of curiosity. Focus on any areas that are weak or entirely absent from your repertoire to begin fostering more curiosity in your life.

A Hundred Questions

Gelb has described a number of exercises in his book to help you develop your curiosity beyond its current level. The first, which sounds easier than it is, is to make a list of 100 questions that you deem significant in your life. Write them down quickly, don't self-censor, and keep going until you have 100 of them. You can do it over several sittings, but keep at it until you have a complete list. Refrain from trying to answer the questions as you write them. Remember the Law of Attraction. Simply asking the questions is enough to draw the answers to you. Let the universe help you with the answers, and remember, it works on its own time schedule. Just to get you started, here are a few from my list...

- How can I have more fun?
- How can I save more money?
- Why do my cats fight with one another?
- When am I most naturally myself?
- What is one thing that I could start or stop doing to improve my life?
- What legacy would I like to leave?
- How can I best be of service to others?
- Why am I overweight?
- How am I perceived by others?

- Am I conceited?
- Is my sense of humor perverse?
- What are the best blessings in my life?
- Why are some people so mean and angry?
- Why do I miss my mom so much?

Notice that some questions are rather deep, and others are lighthearted and downright silly. It takes a lot of thought to come up with 100 questions, so don't feel that they all have to be solemn and serious. Have some fun with this. You will feel your brain stretching as you do the exercise!

Next, isolate the ten most powerful questions on your list and copy them here in order of their importance to your growth and happiness, with the first question being the most important one.

I hope you picked at least a few fun questions to explore! Now that you have isolated your ten most powerful questions, get to work on them. Think about them, and research to find the answers. Ask your friends for feedback about how they handled similar questions in their lives. Google some answers and see what you find. Whatever action you take, remember that the Law of Attraction is at play here and you will attract to yourself the answers you think about and research the most. Don't worry about the remaining 90 questions on your list of 100 questions, just let them marinate, and review the list occasionally. Even without taking action on them I am willing to bet that you will notice the answers coming into your consciousness.

We always find what we are looking for in life. People who seek to be happy usually find that they are, while people who look for misery in every situation are sure to find it as well.

Root Cause Analysis

When I first renewed my focus on curiosity I must admit that I got myself into a bit of trouble. I would think, "I wonder what would happen if I did this, or said that?" and then I would throw caution to the wind and proceed to do or say whatever it was I wanted. Life without filters was fun for me, but perhaps less fun for those around me. I have since refined my process and I now conduct a brief root cause analysis to assess the risk to myself and others from my acting on my unbridled curiosity. It causes me to look at and question my assumptions, some of which may be faulty.

A root cause analysis is a process by which you ask the question, "Why?" seven times before you implement an intended action. This process involves drilling down to find the root cause of the situation or problem that you are facing. Once you discover the primary cause of a situation you will get straight to the solution instead of wasting time addressing the symptoms of the issue at hand. Here is an example of how a root cause analysis might go.

Question 1: Why are we so mean and angry at work?
Answer: Because we are frustrated with the work overload and no one likes one another.
Question 2: Why do we have a work overload and why don't we like each other?
Answer: Because people spend more time complaining about the workload than addressing it, and because we are quick to gossip and believe the worst about one another.
Question 3: Why can't we get this situation under control and be happier and more productive at work?
Answer: Because we are in the habit of griping and we don't trust one another or management.
Question 4: Why don't we trust one another and why do we enjoy speaking ill of each other?

Answer: Because it is more fun to be mean than to be nice at work. Being upset and angry gets more attention than being calm or nice. Constantly being mean and angry with one another interferes with building trusting relationships.

Question 5: Why can't we make a conscious effort to be nicer to each other and work to rebuild trust?

Answer: Because some people refuse to trust again after they have been betrayed or hurt by someone else.

Question 6: Why don't I try anyway and see if I can get some people to respond in kind to my efforts?

Answer: Because I am afraid it won't work and everyone will remain angry and lacking in trust.

Question 7: Why won't it work?

Answer: It might. I will try being kinder to others, refrain from gossiping myself or listening to mean gossip about others and see if I can get a few people to be less mean and angry, and to trust me more.

This example may seem rather trivial, but often times we don't take the time to figure out what is really going on in a situation. Root cause analysis allows you to focus your curiosity methodically and look beyond the obvious to find a reasoned response. It allows you to identify and factor in the risks involved with taking action, and keeps your responses anchored in reality.

In short, exercising curiosity will open up a richer world to you. You will notice opportunities where you never dared see them before. Cultivating curiosity will cause you to think more deeply, explore more fully, and live more wide awake than you have ever been before.

Be Curious about Others

Thus far we have discussed you…how to better understand yourself, how to value yourself more, how to make better decisions for yourself, how to be more authentically and uniquely you. But your life can only improve to the extent that others around you allow it. If you have a persistently mouthy child, or a bitter spouse, or a domineering mother you might still find that you need an unfaltering determination to remain consistently happy and at peace with your own life.

The root cause analysis can be helpful when you are assisting others in making good decisions for themselves that may also end up benefitting you. Please know that I am not suggesting that you stick your nose in the business of others, but when they bring up an issue to you, there is no reason why you should hesitate to explore it with them. Especially when others want to control your life or your time, you have both the right and the responsibility to ask why…up to seven times!

The next time someone decides to "should" on you, respond with a root cause analysis. "Should on me?" you might ask. Yes, it happens when someone decides that it would be a good idea for you to be more like them, so they suggest what you "should do." When their unsolicited advice leaves you feeling vaguely guilty you know you have been "should on." There is only one reason to use the word should, and that is to make others feel guilty. It is a mild manipulation that has the potential to lead you in a direction that you don't want to go.

Joan confided in me that her mother was driving her crazy. Every Saturday night, just about the time she and her husband settled in to watch a movie, her mother would call. The call content never varied. Mother would begin by asking, "Are you going to church tomorrow?" Joan would reply in the negative, prompting her mother to begin lecturing her about the pitfalls of being a heathen. I suggested that next Saturday night Joan could refrain from answering her mom and simply ask "Why?" a few times. By doing so she discovered that her mother was less concerned about her becoming a heathen than the harsh comments her church mates would make about her inability to get her family to church. "Ask why that concerns them so," Joan suggested.

The following Saturday Joan was able to enjoy her Saturday evening without a call from her mother. On Sunday evening she called to check on her mom, and to thank her for not putting her on the spot about going to church. "It was the best Sunday ever," her mom reported. "I asked my friends why they were concerned about you not being at church, and they said that they felt sorry for me because I had no one to enjoy the service with." She let them know that sitting alone didn't interfere with the joy she felt while engaged in worship, and felt confident that they wouldn't question Joan's absence in the future.

Beyond helping others think through their expectations of you, a natural inquisitiveness and keen curiosity about others can help you build more lasting relationships. It is hard to say how many divorces have been born of sheer boredom. The old adage, "Familiarity breeds contempt" implies that the better you know someone the less you will like them. I believe the converse can be true as well. Believing you know all there is to know about another person limits your future possibilities together and makes for a dulled relationship. Discovering something new about your friends and family on an ongoing basis keeps the relationship fresh, and your respect for one another robust. Use your newly refreshed sense of curiosity to explore more dimensions of those you know well, and to find out more about people that you would like to get to know better.

Share your list of 100 questions with your mate, your parents, your children, or your closest friend. Ask them to make a list to share with you. Offer to help them answer their questions, and allow them to help you answer yours. Consider making a joint list of questions to research together. It is impossible to outgrow others in your life if you are learning and growing together.

A Real Woman

Cary is the life of every party…fun, funny and smart. Her friends have let her know, however, that they find her fiancé to be a real drag. At social gatherings Tom can be found in a corner, texting on his phone or dozing off. Although Cary makes jokes about Tom's lack of interest in having a social life, it troubles her as well. Lately she has noticed that they generally sit silently while riding in the car or having a meal together. With their interest in one another waning, Cary wonders why they still plan to marry. "Is it possible to continue to love someone who is boring and bored," she wonders.

In an effort to revitalize their relationship Cary proposed a game of Truth or Dare at dinner one evening. By the end of the game Cary was pleasantly surprised by how much she had learned about Tom, his thinking, his attitudes, his past experiences and his future aspirations. Since the game Cary has made it a point to be more curious about the things that interest Tom. She asks more questions about his take on things, and remembers to share items that she hears or reads during her day that she thinks might interest him. Conversely, Tom has also seems to take a greater interest in Cary now and makes an effort at social gatherings to be more involved. It seems that once Cary experienced Tom as a more interesting person he began to feel like one. Knowing that he has something to contribute to the conversation has brought Tom out of his shell. Cary's friends have quit commenting, "I don't know what you see him," because now they see it too.

Beautify Your Body

"Take care of your body. It's the only place you have to live." Jim Rohn

I have never met a woman who didn't want to be beautiful. Sadly, I have only met a few women who believe that they actually are. From the time we are tiny girls we are sent messages about how we look. We are compared mercilessly to our classmates and cousins, asked to focus on the assets that they possess that we do not. Are you too short, too fat, too skinny, shaped oddly, suffering from "cankles," heavily featured, with bad hair and an uneven complexion? Maybe your neck is too long or your fingers are crooked. Perhaps your ears are too big, or your bust is too small. Regardless of the feature you are over or under endowed with, you have probably been lamenting the flaw since childhood.

Recently I was doing my hair and make-up in the locker room of our local YMCA. A young mother, her infant son and three-year-old daughter sat nearby where I could easily overhear their conversation. The little girl was tired and crabby, finding one thing after another to whine and cry about. Her mother was beginning to lose patience with her when the child approached the mirror beside me to examine her own face. "My nose is too big!" she announced to her mother and I. Before I had time to react her mother broke into a big smile and scooped the little girl into her arms. "You have a beautiful, perfect nose, a nose just like your grandma's nose! I love your nose," she proclaimed showering the child's face with kisses.

Wouldn't it be wonderful if every girl or woman on the planet had this experience? Think of how many of us would love our noses, or thighs, or knees or necks if we just had one other person who thought whatever body part we loathed was "beautiful and perfect." But alas, that is usually not our experience. Advertisers tell us daily that there is something inherently wrong with who we are in our natural state. We are bombarded with ads that push products to rid ourselves of embarrassing hair, age spots, cellulite, varicose veins, bags, sags, wrinkles and ruin. We are encouraged to wear Spanks, tummy control jeans, bras that lift and separate, shoes that force our feet into pointy toes, and bathing suits that flatter your particular shape. Never mind the discomfort associated with these torture devices, because we all know that you must suffer to be beautiful.

Mirrors become our enemy, and every time we see one we focus on what is wrong, rather than what is attractive about the person before us. In the extreme we will also become hyper-critical of close family members insisting that the spouse and kids must also present a perfect image lest others blame us for their poor appearance. For some, how they look becomes more important than how they feel. Comfort is sacrificed, and dignity becomes dependent on how you and others think you look. Kind of nuts, isn't it?

Wayne Dyer, one of my favorite self-help gurus gives great advice when it comes to beautifying your body. "Begin to see yourself as a soul with a body rather than a body with a soul," Dyer advises. In short, beauty comes from the inside out. Spiritual, emotional and physiological beauty all begins with an internal makeover rather than an exterior one. Have you ever seen a woman who glows? She has a bounce in her step, an expression of calm on her face, and moves with a grace that eludes ordinary humans. Regardless of her hair texture, ankle girth or skin tone, she is beautiful, and she knows it. She radiates health and gives off an energy that can't be purchased at the makeup counter of even the best department store.

I wish there was a magic potion that I could recommend to bring about the vitality I am describing, but I don't believe such a substance exists. The key to internal and external beauty lies in three time-tested strategies: meditation, diet and exercise.

Meditation

Meditation gives you access to your soul, the true source of your power and beauty. Put aside at least 15 minutes daily to meditate. Thirty minutes is even better if you can squeeze out the time. Meditation just before bed can do double duty to relax you and put positive thoughts in your mind that will lead to pleasant dreams. Buddha was asked, "What have you gained from meditation?" He replied, "Nothing, however let me tell you what I have lost; anger, anxiety, depression, insecurity, fear of old age and death."

To meditate effectively you must be in a quiet place and in a comfortable position. Your first task is to completely relax. Many of us don't know how to fully relax and we carry tension in our muscles most all of the time, even while we sleep. To let go of the tension you will begin by doing a "body walk." Begin with your feet. Curl your toes. Hold the tension for five seconds and release. Now point your toes to the ceiling. Hold for five seconds, and release. Now your feet and calves are relaxed. Move on to your thighs. Press them together, hold, then release. Now tense the muscles in your buttocks. Hold and release. Next raise your arms about three inches from where they are resting. Hold and release. Hunch your shoulder, hold and release. Now point your chin towards the ceiling...hold, release. Finally scrunch up your face in a big frown. Release the tension from your face. Take a deep cleansing breath, in through your nose and out through your mouth. Envision yourself blowing any remaining tension away from your body. Your entire body should now be completely relaxed and you are ready to begin your meditation.

Continue breathing slowing and deliberately. Feel the oxygen nourishing your cells and energizing your brain. Close your eyes. Envision yourself in a place of natural beauty. Soak in the atmosphere, feel the breeze in your hair and the sun on your face. Immerse yourself in the beauty and the calm. Once you are deeply relaxed ask the cosmic a question, really anything that you would like an answer to. Where will I find true love? What do I need to do to afford college? How can I attract more good things into my life? Wait patiently for the answers that will come in the form of ideas or inspirations. Your answers may not come immediately but within a few days you will begin to hear, see, think about, and/or feel, the answers that you seek.

Bring yourself gently out of your meditation with another deep cleansing breath. Spend a moment or two considering how you feel. Notice the benefits to your body and mind of the deep state of relaxation you have achieved. Your muscles are no longer achy and tense, your facial tension is gone, and your teeth are unclenched. You feel warm and safe and serene. Enjoy the lovely sensations.

That all sounds pretty good, but what does it have to do with becoming more beautiful? Being able to relax and focus on what you want in life has everything to do with your attractiveness. Relaxed, confident people are always perceived to be more beautiful than those who are anxious and worried. Look at the faces of the middle aged and senior women you know. Notice that their whole life is written on their face. If they have spent a lifetime wearing a frown their worry lines will be deep. Some will look hard and haggard. Others however, those who have lived lives filled with joy, peace and happiness will look soft, radiant and even a little twinkly! Shedding the stress in your life, and learning to dedicate a portion of each day to relaxation can improve your posture, reduce the level of chronic pain that you carry, and help you move with more grace and ease by staving off arthritis, muscle strain and accidents caused by being rushed and unfocused. We will talk more about stress management in another chapter of this e-book, but for now, know that learning to relax can not only add years to your life, but it can improve your looks as well.

Diet

Eating right can be the difference between looking and feeling great, and dragging around hungry and sluggish. Even if your weight is within an acceptable range what you eat can boost your energy levels and provide you with a vitality that makes you look and feel more attractive.

According to the Centers for Disease Control (CDC), 35.7% of Americans are obese. Obesity-related conditions include heart disease, stroke, type 2 diabetes and certain types of cancer, some of the leading causes of preventable death. An adult who has a Body Mass Index (BMI) of 30 or higher is considered obese. A BMI of 18.5 to 24.9 is considered a healthy weight. To both look and feel better most of us need to lose a little weight and build a bit more muscle tone so there isn't quite as much bounce to the ounce.

Dieting is a multi-million dollar industry in the U. S. although it is widely accepted that diets don't work in the long term. Most dieters end up in a yo-yo pattern of losing and regaining weight that is ultimately more detrimental than just remaining overweight. In order to look and feel better for life you need to adopt an eating philosophy that allows you to consume sensibly without feeling deprived or depraved! My Plate is a new representation by the USDA to illustrate how much you need to eat of each food group daily. Lots of veggies (unlimited) and fruits (2-3 servings), at least half of your grains (2-3 servings) should be whole grains, low-fat or no fat dairy, and 2-3 helpings of protein daily.

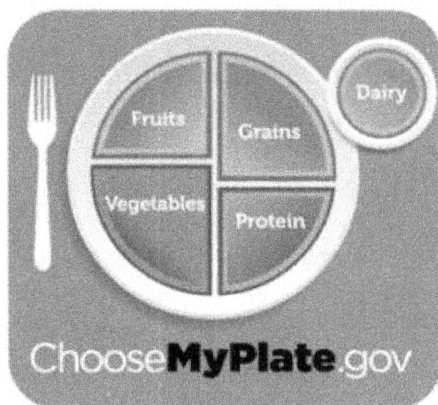

In short, if it grows you can eat it. If it is manufactured or processed you should limit your intake of it. A balanced diet augmented a time or two weekly with a dessert or some junk food will help you maintain a clear complexion, bright eyes, and a healthy body weight. My aunt's rule, "All things in moderation." is a good guideline to apply to your dietary intake. A little alcohol (a daily glass of wine) can also help with digestion and make a balanced diet a bit more fun. Just count it as a helping of fruit, and delete it from your diet if you are pregnant or nursing. If you have health conditions that require you to have a special diet be sure to check with your doctor before modifying your food intake. Some medications don't mix well with certain food, and your doctor may direct you to avoid otherwise healthy foods like grapefruit or leafy green veggies if they would interact badly with your medicine.

Exercise

If you are like me just the mere word "exercise" makes you feel sore all over. Even those of us who exercise regularly will usually admit that this is something one forces oneself to do. The wonderful thing that I and others have discovered though is that a few hours of exercise each week does more to make us feel good, look good and stay healthy than anything else. Exercising the body helps clear your mind, relieve stress, staves off age related conditions such as arthritis, and builds muscle tone needed to move gracefully and give your body its best shape. The trick is to find activities you enjoy and engage in them regularly.

I am a swimmer. It is a super full body workout that can be accomplished without sweating. It is ideal for a woman my age who wants a low-impact workout that promotes cardio-vascular health without pounding your joints or straining your muscles. Water aerobics can get the same results if you like water but can't swim. Mixing the two will give your workouts a bit of variety and allows you to do spot work on particular muscle groups that you wish to strengthen.

Walking, bicycling, spinning, dancing, WII Fit and using an elliptical machine are other options if you wish to burn a few calories, stay active and shape your body. For those who want to do something more strenuous, try High Intensity Training (HIT) where you use either free weights or a recumbent bike to do seven bouts of extremely fast, difficult exercise, each round lasting 30-45 seconds with 60-90 seconds of rest between the sprints. HIT gives you great muscle definition and a good cardio workout in a very short time (20 minutes 2-3 times each week) and it has a high fat burning effect as well.

In order to decide what to include in your exercise routine, do three things. First (and this one is difficult), stand naked before your mirror and study your profile, front, back and from the side. What areas of your body need to gain better muscle tone or definition? How is your posture? Take your weight and measurements (upper arms, bust, waist, hips thighs and calves) and record them. Now you have a baseline that you can use to measure your progress over time.

Second, ask your doctor's advice. S/he will tell you how strenuously to exercise based on your health and current level of conditioning. Third, take the assessment on the next page to explore your options and assure that you develop an exercise plan that is suited to you and that you will find fun and interesting. The more enjoyable the activity is for you the more likely it is that you will stick with it.

The assessment has been adapted from the article *Find the Best Workout for You* by Annabelle Robertson at Web MD.

About You	Yes	No	Suggestions if you checked "Yes"
Do you hate the gym?			Take a walk, ride a bike, or go for a hike, exercise in a park using your own body weight." Ideas include pushups, squats, squat jumps, crunches, and planks. Consider outdoor group classes
Are you seriously out of shape?			Exergames like Wii Fit, or wear a pedometer and make it a goal to take more and more steps each day, with the goal of getting up to 8,000 to 10,000 steps per day, start walking 10 minutes daily and work up to 30 minutes
Are you sociable and would like to meet new people and make new friends?			Dancing and yoga are among the most popular group activities. Try Zumba, salsa, ballroom, hip hop, or country line dancing. There are a number of types of yoga—start simple and gradually move to more challenging routines
Do you need some pointers or someone to hold you accountable?			Hire a personal trainer who is certified by the American Council of Sports Medicine (ACSM). If you can't afford private sessions, consider teaming up with a friend or two -- or taking a group exercise class conducted by a trainer
Do you need some tough love to motivate you to push yourself?			Boot camps are an option that might suit you, especially if you're motivated by someone yelling at you
Are you pressed for time?			Try working out at your desk. Do dips on your chair. Drop down and do some pushups off the edge of your desk. Get some resistance bands and do bicep curls and tricep extensions
Are you on a tight budget?			Buy a few resistance bands, some dumbbells, and a stability ball to create unlimited workouts at home. Try squats, multi-planar lunges, push-ups, walking lunges with torso rotations, long jumps, bridges with knee extensions, or walking on all fours, all free of charge!

Do you need a challenge?			Take whatever you're already doing to the next level. If you're into strength training, sign up for a body building show. If you're into cardio, do an endurance event like a half marathon or marathon. Set a goal and go for it!
Do you have trouble touching your toes?			Stretching increases range of motion, allowing you to perform more exercises, with better results. Stretches should be held for 20 to 30 seconds each – with no bouncing. Another option is classes such as yoga, Pilates, or tai chi that will work toward increasing your flexibility
Are you easily bored?			Look for cross training options such as cycling, swimming, and running. Bryant recommends changing your main activity every six to eight weeks. Alternatively, you can mix up each workout.

Energy

Becoming healthier through meditation, restful sleep, good nutrition and exercise will cause you to feel more energetic. People who exude energy are generally viewed as being more attractive than those who are lethargic and depressed. Move faster and move more throughout your day to keep your energy level high. Despite your best efforts you may still feel worn out by mid-afternoon, especially if you have a job that keeps you stationary. Physics are at play here. Newton's First Law states "An object at rest will remain at rest unless acted on by an unbalanced force. An object in motion continues in motion with the same speed and in the same direction unless acted upon by an unbalanced force." This law is often called "the law of inertia". When you find yourself the victim of inertia move around if possible, and breathe. Here are a few breathing techniques that can be done at your desk, in your car, in a restroom stall, or while lying down to help you balance your energy level.

To increase sagging energy levels:

❑ Take a deep cleansing breath in through your nose & out through your mouth
❑ Take in a second breath through your nose & hold it deep in your lungs for as long as you can (30-40 seconds).
❑ Expel the breath through your mouth blowing beyond the point that your lungs feel completely empty.
❑ Take in a third breath and repeat the holding & expelling process. Continue until you have held a total of six breaths.
❑ Finish with another cleansing breath and notice how much warmer and more awake and energetic you feel.

To calm yourself down:

❑ Take a deep cleansing breath in through your nose & out through your mouth
❑ Take in a second breath through your nose and expel it slowly in two parts saying Paah-Paah as you breathe out.
❑ Repeat the breathing pattern six times in a waltz rhythm (uhm-paah-paah, uhm on the inhale, paah-paah on the exhale).
❑ Finish with a cleansing breath and notice how much calmer and relaxed you feel.
❑ You may augment this exercise by closing your eyes and envisioning yourself in your favorite tranquil place as you breathe.

To better focus your thoughts:

- ❑ Take a deep cleansing breath in through your nose & out through your mouth
- ❑ Take a second long slow breath through your nose and hold it for five seconds.
- ❑ Expel the breath slowly and then take in the next breath.
- ❑ Repeat the breathing pattern six times and finish with a cleansing breath.
- ❑ While doing the exercise envision the best outcome possible to the situation you are thinking about.
- ❑ Notice how many more options you can generate after you have increased the oxygen supply your brain needs to function efficiently.

Reduce your Bad Habits

So far in this book we have discussed things that will help you feel better, look better and be better. Now let's discuss things that make you feel, look and be worse. The lesser world that we live in tends to pull us down from time to time. During these times we develop bad habits. Smoking, drinking, doing recreational drugs or mood altering prescription drugs, over-eating, over-caffeinating, watching too much TV, hiding out in your bedroom, failing to maintain your hygiene routines, really any behavior that makes you feel good for a few minutes and feel guilty continuously.

Think about it this way. Whenever you allow yourself to do something that you know is not in your best interest you are giving your power away to that thing. In essence you are saying that this thing, whatever it may be, is more important and more powerful than your own will. Crazy, isn't it?

Here are three specific strategies you can use to avoid bad habits, take back your power, and do what you need to do to keep yourself healthy, vibrant and energetic.

1. Don't think about it, just do it! If you think too much about whether you want to go jogging, or pass up that extra cocktail you will almost always decide against it. No one *wants* to do things that are difficult for us, and the more you consider your options the more likely you are to choose what you want to do rather than what you need to do.
2. Think about the good result you attain if you do the thing you need to do. Say to yourself, "I always feel wonderful after a jog," or "I will awake without a hangover tomorrow if I pass on this extra dose of alcohol that is tempting me."
3. Start small. Instead of jogging for an hour commit to jogging for 15 minutes. Resist that extra drink for 30 minutes. You will find that once you get started on something you are dreading, or resist a momentary temptation, the momentum will build and you will get caught up in doing the right thing. Keeping with our example, you may end up jogging for 45 minutes instead of the 15 minutes you set as a goal, and that extra drink will be completely forgotten if you delay pouring it.

Take a few minutes and think about the bad habits you are currently indulging. Write them on the chart. Beside each habit listed say what you will do instead of becoming powerless when tempted. Read this chart daily to remind yourself of your new thinking and behavior until your old habits are replaced by other activities that make you happier and healthier.

Bad Habit   **New Healthy Habit**
1.
2.
3.
4.

Pampering

You were probably taught to be attentive to others and that your own needs are secondary to their needs. The kids, the spouse, local charities and even your friends seem to take up all of your time and money. There is little left for you, and even if you do decide to do something nice for yourself you may find yourself feeling guilty about treating yourself, thereby destroying the benefits you hoped to derive from your moment of self-indulgence. Just a little advice...get over it!

Pampering yourself is not a luxury, it is a necessity. Investing time and money in your own wants and needs is an investment in your present and your future. A little pampering on a regular basis will bring you immediate happiness and can actually extend your life and promote good health over time. Would you like to get a makeover? Have you been dying to see the new exhibit at the art gallery? The first step is to identify all of the things you have been meaning to do for yourself but haven't. To prepare to pamper yourself in a meaningful way begin by making two lists in the space provided.

Things I Need   **Things I Want**

Start the pampering process by giving yourself one thing you want and one thing you need over the next month. Choose things off your list that are affordable and accessible. Simultaneously, begin saving or planning for something on your list that will be feasible for you to attain in six months if you are diligent in preparing for it. Don't fall into the trap of obtaining only what you need. Incorporate some of what you want as well. It is attaining your wants, even more so than meeting your needs that will help you feel rewarded and cared for.

A Real Woman

Anita awoke sore, out of sorts and worn out again. Her 40th birthday was at hand, but she felt more like she was in her early 60's. She considered going to the doctor, thinking that she might be diagnosed with chronic fatigue syndrome or fibromyalgia. If she did get such a diagnosis she would likely be prescribed medications that she would need to take for the remainder of her life, and she really didn't like the thought of that.

A former high school athlete, Anita was now 30 pounds overweight. Due to her weight she avoided mirrors, and since she was chronically sore she also steered clear of any activity that would result in physical exertion. Anita had always considered herself to be naturally attractive and had never used much makeup or hair color, but when she caught a glimpse of herself in a reflective surface these days she was sad to see an exhausted, washed out woman that she barely recognized.

Anita always resisted when a friend suggested that she join her for Zumba classes and Weight Watcher meetings, but at this point she was nearly out of excuses, so reluctantly she accepted the invitation. Zumba turned out to be great fun and she ran into a couple of friends she hadn't seen in years at the recreation center where the classes and meetings were held. Four months later, toned and thirty pounds thinner, Anita's entire life had changed. She looked and felt young again. She had become active in a number of activities at the rec center which renewed her interest in her own life. She signed on to be the sous chef at the healthy cooking class and was looking forward to doing the three-day walk for breast cancer with her new friends.

"I refuse to ever be old again!" Anita was heard to exclaim as she sprinted across the finish line at the end of the breast cancer walk. Now that's the spirit!

Soul Signals

"Music in the soul can be heard by the universe." Lao Tzu

If you have come to this point in this book, and have done all of the assignments, you are to be congratulated on your hard work and personal progress. Thus far we have been sanding away at your fault lines, knowing that women must see, feel and hear about their improvements before they are fully convinced that they have progressed. Men, lucky humans that they are, can become true believers in their own success much more quickly than any female that I have ever known. So take a moment now, and let your progress settle into your conscious mind. It is my fondest wish that you were able to answer with a resounding *yes* to some, if not all of these queries.

	Yes	No
Have you become happier since beginning this book?		
Do you look better?		
Do you feel better?		
Are you more confident?		
Are you better focused?		
Do you feel more motivated and energized?		

If you are unable to respond affirmatively to each question, it may be worthwhile to revisit previous sections of this book and delve a little deeper into area(s) where you are not yet noticing a positive outcome. I know it is tempting to just pick pieces and parts you want to improve, but truly mind, body and soul are inextricably linked and you must attend to all of these aspects of your life if you wish to be fully healthy and happy.

You are now beginning to grow holistically and synergistically. Do you notice how your mind is influencing your body and your body is influencing your mind? They are working together to steel your resolve, to fuel your enthusiasm, and to propel you to greater personal heights than you have attained thus far in your life. Let's advance our discussion now to examine how your soul and your connection to it can enhance or detract from the quality of your life.

The soul is more difficult to discuss than the mind and body. There is little written about the soul in popular literature, probably because few contemporary authors want to take on the subject. Many consider the soul to be a matter of conjecture. How do you think and feel about the soul? Take this assessment to examine your current beliefs.

	Yes	No
Does the soul actually exist?		
Is it possible to know how it functions in our daily lives?		
Is anyone a true expert on this topic?		
Do you have to be a religious person to appreciate the importance of your soul?		
Is it possible to clearly communicate with your soul?		

A discussion of the soul and how it functions is not something that you are likely to converse about at work or with an acquaintance at a social event. It is much too risky to do so. Articulating one's own views on the topic might make others uncomfortable or worse yet, cause you to be perceived as insane!

This book is based primarily on the life lessons I have learned while attempting to be a greater woman in a lesser world. I write this chapter with more hesitancy than I imagined I would. Attempting to find the perfect approach and phrasing to discuss the soul is difficult. I have no desire to offend anyone, yet I am compelled to write this chapter as honestly as possible. My beliefs are evident throughout this discussion, and I invite you to keep an open mind as you consider my views. Some will reject the concepts I embrace, and others will find a source of strength and meaning here. It is for those who will find benefit in my explanation that I tackle the sensitive issue of discussing the soul.

As women, we have all had some experience with the phenomena known as women's intuition. I believe that woman's intuition is nothing more or less than a woman's soul communicating with her. Let's start this discussion on familiar and common ground. Let's examine how and why "woman's intuition" occurs.

Woman's Intuition

Is woman's intuition real or imagined? It is real. But where does it come from? Dr. Daniel Amen, author of _Unleash the Female Brain_ recently conducted the largest brain imaging study ever done. He examined the blood flow and activity patterns in 46,000 male and female brains and in 70 of the 80 tests conducted female brains were more active than those of their male counterparts. Dr. Amen contends that because of this increased activity females often exhibit greater strengths in the areas of empathy, intuition (knowing something that is true without knowing exactly why), collaboration, self-control and appropriate worry.

> Women know. They just know. Even if they didn't know, they would know. Men might not get this, but women will, because they know.

Researchers found that females have more activity in the part of the brain responsible for gut feelings and intuition. Compared to men, women have significantly more activity in the limbic (emotional and bonding areas of the brain), as well as in the prefrontal cortex, an area responsible for planning, judgment, empathy, impulse control, and error detection. It appears the female brain is perfectly suited to receive and respond to the messages our soul communicates to us.

A number of neuroscientists, doctors and philosophers have established a contention between the limbic system, and most particularly the hypothalamus, a gland within the limbic system, and soul communications. Some even postulate that the soul itself resides within the hypothalamus. Perhaps the greater activity in the limbic system of the female brain is responsible for the enhanced sense of soul connection and intuitive power demonstrated by women than by their male counterparts.

Woman's intuition alone cannot explain some of the functions that the female psyche is able to perform. Have you ever had any of these experiences?

	Yes	No
Have you had precognitions where you might dream, or see in your mind's eye a situation that has not yet occurred?		
Do you sometimes know what others are thinking even if you don't know them well?		
Have you experienced deja vu (French for "already seen"), the feeling that you have had the same experience you are currently having at an earlier time?		
Have you ever experienced a sense of dread or foreboding that warns you of impending doom before an incident or accident actually occurs?		
Could it be when these phenomena occur that you are hearing directly from your soul?		

The Soul

What exactly is the soul? The Encyclopedia Britannica defines soul as the immaterial aspect or essence of a human being, that which confers individuality and humanity, often considered to be synonymous with the mind or the self. In theology, the soul is further defined as that part of the individual which partakes of divinity and often is considered to survive the death of the body. In short, your soul is you. Oddly, you may think of yourself as your body, but when you refer to your body, or any of its parts, you say "MY body" or "MY arm" indicating that it belongs to you, but is not you. Your soul is your essence, your being...you.

What If?

What if our religion was each other?
If our practice was our life?
If prayer was our words?
What if the Temple was the Earth?
If forests were our church?
If holy water—the rivers, lakes and oceans?
What if meditation was our relationships?
If the Teacher was Life?
If wisdom was self-knowledge?
If love was the center of our being

∞ love

A poem by Ganga White

And you are not alone. Your soul and all other souls, are part of a collective consciousness that you can access through meditation and/or prayer. Even the souls of those who have died are a part of this collective, and are accessible to you if you know how to listen for their voices.

I consider my soul to be my primary power source. It is my creator living within me, and when I hear the voice of my creator, I hear it through the gateway of my soul. My soul, therefore is the source of my conscience, my goodness, and my ability to love. My soul is ageless and endless. It preceded my present life and will continue after my death. My soul is the source of my creativity, my inspiration, my motivation, and the specific giftedness that I am endowed with.

So your soul, and the care and nurturing of it, is probably your most important function as a human being. It is incumbent upon us to listen to our soul, support it with our thoughts, and manifest it in our behavior. Your soul connects you to your past, and prepares you for your future. Your soul is where your spirit is housed. It is a source of strength for which there is no substitute.

Lately I have noticed that a growing number of my friends are polarized on the issue of religion. About half of those I know are atheist. They believe in evolution as the inception of human life, and feel that when you die you simply cease to exist. Other friends are religious, some fiercely so. They believe that regulating their behavior and living according to the rules of their faith will get them to the Promised Land upon their earthly demise. They tend to think that their "eternity" began on the day they were born. My beliefs don't fall into either camp. I embrace my spirituality.

Here is the rub. Eternity has no beginning and no end. And God is everything, and everybody, including you. God is love. It is all quite expansive, isn't it? You are part of something much grander than yourself, whether you care to acknowledge it or not. But if you decide to, you can use your soul as the gateway to greater awareness and deeper understanding of yourself, others and nature. Atheists can't explain how evolution began, nor can the religious say where or when your soul originated. Your soul has always existed and will continue to exist long after your earthly passing, because it is part of the God consciousness which is eternal. God said, "I am the alpha and the omega," the beginning and the end. If you are a true manifestation of God, then you too are the beginning and the end.

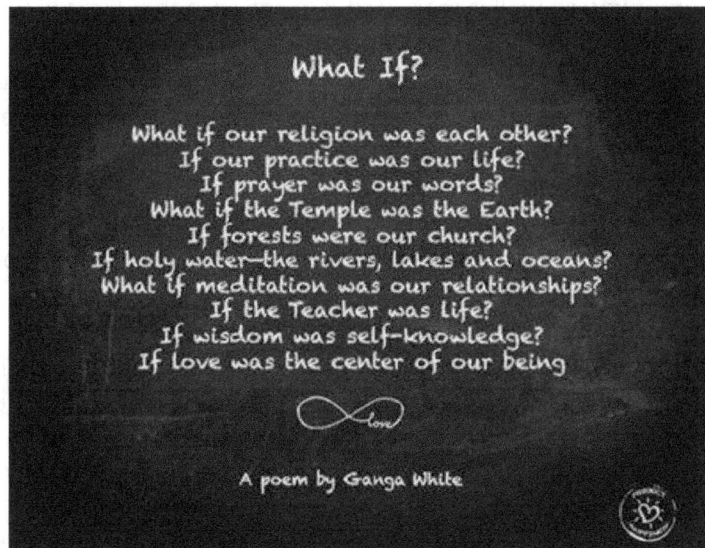

So maybe that deja vu feeling is the remnant of a memory from a previous life, and perhaps the intuition that serves you so well is merely soul experience that kicks in when you need it the most. The only thing I know for sure is that the more I think and behave in concert with my soul, the more harmonious and joyous my life becomes. I feel so blessed to be a woman, because the structure and function of my brain is perfectly aligned with my soul purpose, and it allows me to access soul guidance with such speed that sometimes my thoughts can't keep up with the information my soul is sending.

So how do you access your soul? It hardly seems practical to just sit around hoping that it will kick in when you need it to. Prayer and meditation are two deliberate and focused ways to get in touch with your inner wisdom...your soul.

My favorite Bible verse is a simple one, Psalm 46:10, "Be still and know that I am God." To me this means that you must quiet yourself and listen to the God inside you. Quieting yourself is where meditation comes into play. You began practicing meditation in chapter three, if you are following the instructions in this book. It was suggested that you consult your soul, through meditation, to find answers to the pressing questions in your life. Now we will look at a deeper level of meditation, one that leads to overall soul satisfaction. We will learn how to quiet ourselves...and listen, just listen...without anguish, without seeking answers, without expectation.

A friend emailed me regularly while her father was dying. She was trying to do it all, support her mother, honor her father's wishes, and attend to her own family while making the necessary medical decisions to facilitate her father's passing. Near the end, she revealed that she was "praying incessantly" for guidance. I wrote back and asked that she stop praying, and wait for an answer. Not even God can interrupt a woman who is doing something "incessantly." Her answers came almost instantly when she relinquished control, demonstrated faith, and quieted herself to listen. Letting go of a prayer, and releasing it to your God consciousness is, in itself, an act of faith. It is based on the belief that something or someone with greater wisdom than you will issue a response. A prayer only needs to be said once in order for it to be heard, but sometimes the response to prayer has to be manifested many times before we get the message.

Remember the old joke about a man who was flooded out of his home? It had been raining for days and days, and a terrible flood had come over the land. The waters rose so high that one man was forced to climb onto the roof of his house. As the waters rose higher and higher, a man in a rowboat appeared, and told him to get in. "No," replied the man on the roof. "I have faith in the Lord; the Lord will save me." So the man in the rowboat went away. The man on the roof prayed for God to save him.

The waters rose higher and higher, and suddenly a speedboat appeared. "Climb in!" shouted a man in the boat. "No," replied the man on the roof. "I have faith in the Lord; the Lord will save me." So the man in the speedboat went away. The man on the roof prayed for God to save him.

The waters continued to rise. A helicopter appeared and over the loudspeaker, the pilot announced he would lower a rope to the man on the roof. "No," replied the man on the roof. "I have faith in the Lord; the Lord will save me." So the helicopter went away. The man on the roof prayed for God to save him. The waters rose higher and higher, and eventually they rose so high that the man on the roof was washed away, and alas, the poor man drowned.

Upon arriving in heaven, the man marched straight over to God. "Heavenly Father," he said, "I had faith in you, I prayed to you to save me, and yet you did nothing. Why?" God gave him a puzzled look, and replied "I sent you two boats and a helicopter, what more did you expect?

Yes, you have to listen and watch for the answer to prayer, otherwise you may literally miss the boat!

Listening for Soul Signals

Pir-O-Murshid Hazrat Inayat Khan, is the founder of the Sufi Order. His work is currently presented by *Bowl of Saki,* an inspirational website. Kahn states, "Life is an opportunity given to satisfy the hunger and thirst of the soul." To me, this means we must not just consult our soul in order to find the answers to the thorny issues of life, but we must listen to the God Consciousness to discover the specifics of our soul's appetite. It is akin to looking into the refrigerator, when you know you are hungry, but you aren't sure what you want to eat. If you are lucky you will see the exact thing you want, and you will know immediately that this is the specific food that will satisfy your appetite.

You may find, after following the rather basic instruction given in this book that you will want to delve further into meditative techniques and targets, and you may even want to devote time to the study of one or more philosophical ideologies pertaining to effective soul communication. For our purposes here, however, we will follow what Deepak Chopra calls the *Law of Dharma,* or *The Purpose of Life.* Chopra introduces the topic of Dharma by saying, "Everyone has a purpose in life...a unique gift or a special talent to give to others. And when we blend this unique talent with service to others, we experience ecstasy and exultation of our own spirit, which is the ultimate goal of all goals." He further suggests three meditative focuses to help you satisfy the hunger of your soul.

You were asked to identify your purpose in the first chapter of this book. This soul meditation will help you actualize your purpose by focusing you on how you will use your purpose in service to others.

Soul Meditation

Today and every day lovingly nurture the God that lies deep in your soul. Pay attention to the spirit that animates your body and your mind. Awaken yourself to the deep stillness in your heart, and carry with you the consciousness of the timeless, eternal being that you are in the midst of your time-bound, earthbound experience. List your unique talents.

My unique talents are...

Next, list the things you love to do while expressing your unique talents. When you use your unique talents in service to humanity you lose track of time and create abundance in your life and in the lives of others.

The things I love to do while using my talents are...

Ask yourself, how can I serve? How can I help? The answers you find will allow you to serve yourself and others with love.

How can I serve?

Try it, You'll Like it

Over time, you will become accustom to rising in the morning with this prayer on your mind, "What can I do today to find the good in others and lift it up?" This small query will direct your talents to where they are most needed. I like to ask my soul this question in a variety of situations throughout my day, but it is an automatic practice for me each morning. I follow this query with a request, "Lord, please let me say and do the things that the people I encounter today need to hear and see to enrich their lives." Begin with these two meditations daily to begin communicating purposefully with your soul.

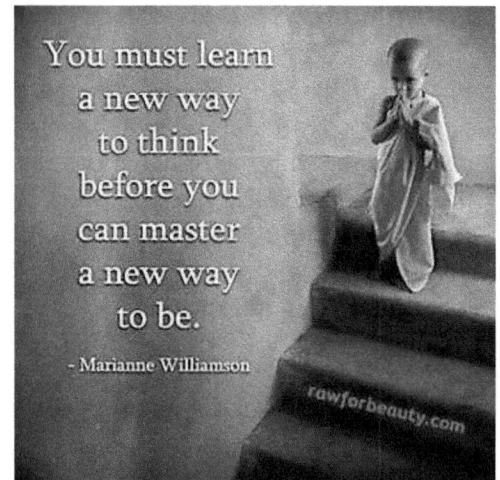

You must learn a new way to think before you can master a new way to be.

- Marianne Williamson

rawforbeauty.com

At least three times weekly set aside time to meditate on the questions posed by Chopra. Relax, breathe, and be still. Experience the peace and wisdom that lie within your God Consciousness. See yourself acting with the confidence and competence derived from using your gifts in a loving way to serve others. Begin to experience yourself from the perspective of what you have to give, rather than to focus on what you need. Meditate on how you can be of more help and service to others. The answers will both astound and delight you.

You will find yourself feeling quite at home with the answers your soul reveals. A "peace that passes understanding" will fill you with hope and excitement. You will arise refreshed and invigorated...ready to take on the world in a new and empowered way.

Karma, Karma, Karma

There have been a number of posters on my Facebook newsfeed lately dealing with the subject of Karma. Most are humorous...*My dream job would be driving the karma bus!* And...*Dear Karma, I have a list of the people you missed!* True enough, it is more fun to think about the Karma others are earning rather than our own. I have one dear friend who insists she doesn't believe in Karma because she never gets to witness others getting theirs. I always reassure her that she doesn't really need to believe in Karma, because it is enough that Karma believes in her.

To begin our discussion of Karma, let's clear up several misconceptions. Karma is neither negative nor positive by nature. It is simply a response to your intentions and behaviors. Someone else's Karma does not need to be delivered by you in order to be effective in addressing their behavior, and many times it occurs but goes unseen by you. Other times you will see it distinctly, and when you do, it is okay for you to be happy that it occurred. It is not okay however, to rejoice at the suffering of others, but just to know that they have received a valuable lesson. If they learn from the lesson, both the person and the world will be better for it, and that is a reason to celebrate.

Karma brings things back into balance, and when you have been wronged you generally feel that things are out of balance. Often, we want to "get even" or "see him get his," to regain the balance that we feel is lacking, but usually retribution does little but earn you some negative Karma of your own. Karma is delivered, in equal proportion to the harm, or good that incurred it, without you ever having to lift a finger. And that is fortunate because you have little control over the person's life who has wronged you. What is in your control is the Karma you are earning for yourself, and that is where your attention should be concentrated.

Chopra explains that the *Law of Karma*, or *Cause and Effect* means that every action generates a force of energy that returns to us in like kind...we reap what we sow, and what goes around comes around. When we choose actions that bring happiness and success to others, the fruit of our Karma is success and happiness.

As you can see, Dharma and Karma go hand in hand. If it is your continuous intention to be helpful to others, you will reap more assistance than you can handle. And if it doesn't happen instantly, don't despair. Remember that your soul is timeless. Things come to you when they are supposed to, more so than when you want them to, or think you need them. Your soul has impeccable timing, and it is the channel through which your Karma is delivered. Wouldn't you agree that it isn't so much what happens to you, as much as how it impacts your feelings and thoughts that counts?

If you have caused someone else to feel defeated, overwhelmed, worthless, or embarrassed, it won't be long before a situation arises that will cause you to react in like manner. If you find yourself wondering why bad things are always happening to you look first at your behavior and intentions towards others to find the answer. It is disappointing when you don't get to see the Karma that others are earning for themselves delivered, but it is a downright shame when you don't recognize your own. Your karmic lessons will just keep coming until you notice and choose to learn from them.

Once you have learned what Karma intends for your to learn, those lessons will stop, and a new set of lessons will replace them. These lessons come in both positive and negative forms, so be sure to notice your positive Karma as well as the negative. Celebrate and extend the great Karma you are earning by passing it along to others, and take the time to enjoy the many blessings that you are reaping. Let your good Karma crowd out your negative intentions and despair. Find something good about everything that occurs in your life. Maintaining an attitude of helpfulness and gratitude will do more to attract positive Karma to your life than any other single act.

The Law of Attraction

One form of Karma is the Law of Attraction. This law, simply stated, says that thoughts are magnetic and that you attract to your life what you think about the most. It is just that simple, and just that complicated at the same time. It is difficult to control your thoughts, and easy to let your doubts drown out the inspiration flowing from your soul. We sometimes come up with great ideas, and clear soul inspirations, and then we proceed to talk ourselves out of them. The "yes, but…" and "what ifs…" that our mind generates can be the source of great internal conflict, and ultimately can interfere with you getting what you want, and what you are meant to receive in this lifetime.

Due to the recent attention the book *The Secret* (2006), by Amanda Byrne has drawn to the Law of Attraction, many believe the law is a new concept. It is an ancient law, an immutable law that has been successfully practiced since early recorded history. Some very wise men have described the Law of Attraction over the centuries. Consider these quotes…

"The ancestor of every action is thought." *Waldo Ralph Emerson*

"All that we are is the result of what we have thought." *Buddha*

"There is nothing neither good nor bad, but thinking makes it so." *William Shakespeare*

"For whatsoever a man sows, that shall he also reap." *The Bible*

"The secret of success lies not without, but within the thoughts of man." *Claude Bristol*

"We become what we contemplate." *George Russell*

"Ideas come from space." *Thomas Edison*

"Self-knowers drink from the fountain of youth, and are at all times owners of what they wish to enjoy."
Paracelsus

What the Law of Attraction means to you...

In the space provided below write a summary of the meaning you derived from reading these quotes. It is only when you fully grasp how the Law of Attraction can work in your life that you will begin to practice it.

The meaning of the Law of Attraction in my life...

The Law of Attraction posits that in order to get ahead and find the fulfillment and happiness you seek, you must engage in creative thinking and hold a firm belief in your ability to execute your ideas. Beyond that, your desire to reach your goal must be obsessive, and your aims must be coordinated so that the soul and the mind are working in concert. Both mental and soul energy must be concentrated on the goal and applied without ceasing.

In his book, *The Magic of Believing* (1948), Claude M. Bristol outlines the steps to be taken to attract into your life the things you desire the most.

1. Determine precisely what you want. State it clearly and decisively.
2. Visualize what your life will be like when you achieve your goal. (I suggest you draw a picture of it to use as a meditation aid.)
3. Write down the specifics of your desired outcome. No detail is too small to note. If you want money, write down the exact amount you are hoping to accumulate. If you want to find the love of your life, describe that person in detail; how they will look, act, think and express love.
4. Decide on the first five steps you will take to begin to take action to achieve your goal. If you wish to attract more money will you need to change jobs, get more education, or perhaps relocate to where employment opportunities are more abundant? If your goal is to find a life mate you might like to work on becoming more like the person you want to attract, or maybe you need to join some organizations where people like you are seeking hang out. You might even want to rid yourself of a few bad habits that have caused you to lose out on relationships in the past.

Remember that you can't control other people, and that to purpose of the Law of Attraction is to fashion yourself, your thoughts, your beliefs and your behavior in such a way that the things and people you want in your life will be attracted to you. You cannot save others from their Karma, for all of us are blessed with free will. Others will do what they want, regardless of our wishes, unless they feel it safe to submit to our influence. You may actually get caught up in someone else's Karma, positive or negative, if you are especially close to them. But, our friend Shakespeare reminds us, "To thine own self be true," regardless of what is going on with those around you. Getting sucked into other's drama, or their good fortune will do little for you. Everything you ever have, or ever hope to have, is something that you earn for yourself through your good deeds, kind intentions, and the relentless pursuit of your own dreams.

A Real Woman

Lela's life was going fine. One might even say that it was "all very well, but not very good." At age 34 she had a job that she didn't hate, an apartment that was small enough to clean in two hours, and a handful of friends that she enjoyed socializing with a couple of times weekly. Her dreams of having a husband, a baby or two, and a house with a lawn were dwindling. At night, before drifting off to sleep she would think about different her life was than she had envisioned it while growing up. "But I am fine and I shouldn't complain," she would think. "At least I am not divorced and trying to be a single parent, like so many women these days."

But it just wouldn't go away, that nagging feeling that her life could be better, and that her dreams could come true. After watching "The Secret" on pay-per-view on a quiet Saturday afternoon she decided to begin putting the principles into action in her own life. She began by writing down what she wanted; a husband who was kind, funny, handsome, and true, children who were joyful, healthy and bright, a boy and a girl, and a house next to a pond, hidden from the road by a grove of trees. She began to draw pictures of the house she envisioned from all angles, each picture featuring one member of her future family. She posted the pictures strategically throughout her small apartment, inside the linen closet, over the sink, anywhere that she might happen upon it during the course of her day. Each evening she engaged in meditative listening, waiting for her soul to inspire her next move.

Two weeks later she noticed a new book store had opened next door to the produce market she was about to enter. On a whim, she decided to stop in and look for something to read poolside later in the day. "What a cool store," she spoke aloud as she admired the cozy atmosphere of the shop. "Why thank you," she heard a warm male voice reply. She whirled around and almost collided with Adam, the shop owner, a man who looked remarkably like the husband in her pictures.

The attraction between the two of them was instant. Six months later they were married and they had two children within the next two years. House hunting was easy for the pair because they narrowed their search to houses with woods and ponds. Two months after their search began the house in Lela's drawing appeared on a realty search website and they purchased it immediately. Is life perfect for Lela and Adam? Of course not, because life is never perfect, but together they are projecting for their next big endeavor, a chain of book stores to be located next to whole foods markets, where the gourmet coffee is free and the sofas are comfy. I bet you can't wait to visit a location near you!

Soulmates

"Real love is a permanently self-enlarging experience." M. Scott Peck

Dear Human: You've got it all wrong. You didn't come here to master unconditional love. That is where you came from and where you'll return. You came here to learn personal love. Universal love. Messy love. Sweaty love. Crazy love. Broken love. Whole love. Infused with divinity. Lived through the grace of stumbling. Demonstrated through the beauty of... messing up. Often. You didn't come here to be perfect. You already are. You came here to be gorgeously human. Flawed and fabulous. And then to rise again into remembering.

So what is love? God's love is unconditional, perfect love. God loves us in abundance as it indicates on the poster at the start of this chapter, but humans simply aren't equipped to master perfect love in one short lifetime. That doesn't, however, keep us from trying. Nothing evolves our soul better, and makes us better people than to master as deep an understanding of human love as is possible. And nothing makes us happier as humans than falling in love.

Dictionary.com defines love as 1) a profoundly tender, passionate affection for another person; 2) a feeling of warm personal attachment or deep affection; 3) sexual passion or desire. I agree with the stated definition, but the order is which the elements of love are presented may need a little rearrangement. Often sexual attraction precedes profound feelings of tenderness or deep personal attachment.

The Law of Attraction is at play at the inception of every romantic relationship. Helen Fisher, PhD, in her article *The Realities of Love at First Sight* reveals that we regularly make up our minds about whether an individual could be an appropriate match for us within the first three minutes of talking to him (or her). It takes less than one second to decide whether you find someone physically attractive. If, however, s/he fits your general concept of what is attractive, your mind races toward the next consideration, voice. Once again, you respond in seconds. Women typically regard rapid talkers as more educated and men with full, deep voices as better-looking than they are. Finally, we listen to his words to decide whether he is intelligent, and to ascertain whether his interests, beliefs and philosophies dovetail nicely with our own.

Despite this, according to a 2003 Gallup poll, only about 40% of all Americans believe in love at first sight. Men believe it occurs more often than do women, and younger people report a stronger belief in it than those over 50. In fact, we may learn as we get older that love at first sight is actually more about lust at first sight. If a woman's brain stops working after checking out appearance and voice characteristics, she may find later that his words, beliefs and philosophies deserved more initial attention!

Every species on the planet has a strong drive to procreate and thus propagate the continuation of their own species, and humans are no exception. The Law of Attraction applies to the functions of the mind, body and soul, although the urge to satisfy the basic needs of the body consistently seem to win out over mind and soul considerations at the onset of a relationship. Ironically, couples in long term relationships find that it is mind and soul compatibility that makes for a durable relationship. The importance of their partner's physical and sexual attractiveness needs tend to wane over time. If you judge another on sexual attraction alone you may find that when the blush falls off the bloom you are left with a mate that you can barely tolerate, so choose holistically if your goal is to find a mate for life.

In her Psychology Today article *Emotional Freedom*, Dr. Judith Orloff clarifies the differences between love and lust. In short, lust may lead to love, but lust alone is characterized as being all about the physical contact between you and your new mate. Signs of love include wanting to spend quality time together other than sex, getting lost in conversations and forgetting about the hours passing, caring about each other's feelings, and wanting to meet one another's family and friends. Being in love with the new mate motivates you to be a better person.

Dr. Orloff has created a list of four ways to know if you should end a relationship before it really gets started.

1. A little voice in your gut says "danger" or "beware."
2. You have a sense of malaise, discomfort, or feeling drained after you're together.
3. Your attraction feels destructive or dark.
4. You're uncomfortable with how this person is treating you, but you're afraid that if you mention it, you'll push him or her away.

In other words, if your mind and your soul are screaming "Nooooooo!" while your body is cooing "Yessssss!" you may want to put your relationship in its proper perspective. Remember, all things that are purely physical are temporary.

Remember, your soul is eternal but your body temporary. Think of it as simply the suit you wear to earth school. When you ask people who have met their soulmates how they knew that other person was really their soulmate they often respond, "It just seemed like I had known him/her forever." In all likelihood they probably have known that person forever.

Soulmates

I am so fortunate to be married to my soulmate. In the chapter of the book _Health Mind Body Soul_ we co-authored Lou and I describe the process that we used to bond with one another and create a lasting relationship. After finding ourselves strongly attracted to one another based on our undeniable chemistry, we began to discuss our spiritual beliefs and found that we both had beliefs that were congruent with one another yet rarely held by mainstream society. Next we tackled politics, educational goals, and personal aspirations. Again, we noticed that we were the same flavor of crazy! We knew early on that we were ideally suited for one another. Although our journey together has been wrought with potholes and puddles, we are still together nearly a quarter of a century later, and we still know that it was meant to be, and we feel certain that we will be together through all eternity. Our story is one of starting in lust, falling in love, being in love, and growing more loving with each passing year.

> _"Important encounters are planned by the souls long before the bodies see each other."_
>
> **~Paulo Coelho**

I have learned a lot from Lou, and he from me. He has changed to be more compatible with me, and I have adapted in a number of areas to be more compatible with him. We both feel that the changes we each chose to make to sustain our relationship have added to each of us, without either of us losing anything valuable in the process. Although we are both fiercely independent people we cannot imagine life without the other. We truly complete one another. Early on, however, we had to get past our idealized notions about what it meant to be in a relationship before we were able to settle into the strong bond we now possess. I now term the foolish notions we embraced our five stupid relationship myths!

Five Stupid Relationship Myths

1. I can make my mate happy and s/he can make me happy! No you can't. You can't make him/her happy, mad, sad or glad nor can they influence your mood if you chose not to allow them to. Each individual chooses how they will respond to the words and actions of another. You can create an environment that

you think your mate might like, but you cannot compel them to react to it the way you hope that they might.

2. I can change my mate. No, it's not happening. If you find something intolerable about your mate you either have to learn to live with it, or leave. S/he has the right to be uniquely themselves and will be so until they decide to alter it, grow past it, or abandon it. You can request that your mate change an aspect of themselves, but demanding it is usually a useless endeavor.

3. If we fight it means we don't love each other. Hogwash! Sometimes you must love each other at the top of your lungs! If two people agree on absolutely everything, one of them is unnecessary. Disagreement leads to learning and growth. If you find yourself fighting more than you find yourself living in harmony, use your natural curiosity to find more things about your mate that you can support, but don't let sporadic anger destroy your ability to love each other!

4. If my friends and family don't like my mate we are doomed. It is always easier if your friends and family support your union, but sometimes negative notions like jealousy, racism, homophobia, class-based prejudice, envy and pride get in the way of others being able to see the positive aspects of your relationship. Remember, this is your soulmate, not theirs, so you really can't expect them to appreciate his/her finer points like you do!

5. My mate will never deliberately hurt me. Yes, s/he will. Humans lash out. They are inherently selfish, and they are known to put their own wants and needs first. Your mate will say hurtful things to you, or will act in ways that betray you, and you will do the same to him/her, but you can get past most any act of betrayal or hurt if you are both committed to better behavior in the future. It won't be easy, but it will probably be worth it.

The 10 Elements of a Soul Mate

So how can you tell if someone is your soul mate, or just a pretender? Dr. Carmen Harra provides us with _The 10 Elements of a Soul Mate_ to help you vet a potential or current mate.

1. **It's something inside.** Describing how a soul mate makes you feel is difficult. It's a tenacious, profound and lingering emotion which no words can encompass.

2. **Flashbacks.** If your partner is your soul mate, chances are he or she has been present in your past lives. You might even feel an odd sense of déjà vu, as if the moment in time has already taken place, perhaps a long time ago, perhaps in a different setting.

3. **You just get each other.** Ever met two people who finish each other's sentences? Some people call that spending too much time together, but I call it a soul mate connection. You might experience this with your best friend or your mother, but it is the telltale sign of a soul mate when you experience it with your partner.

4. **You fall in love with his (or her) flaws.** No relationship is perfect, and even soul mate relationships will experience ups and downs. Still, that bond will be much harder to break. Soul mates have an easier time of accepting, even learning to love, each other's imperfections.

5. **It's intense.** A soul mate relationship may be more intense than normal relationships, in both good and sometimes bad ways. The most important thing is that, even during negative episodes, you're focused on resolving the problem and can see beyond the bad moment.

6. **You two against the world.** Soul mates often see their relationship as "us against the world." They feel so linked together that they're ready and willing to take on any feat of life, so long as they have their soul mate by their side.

7. **You're mentally inseparable.** Soul mates often have a mental connection similar to twins. They might pick up the phone to call each other at the exact same time. Though life may keep you apart at times, your minds will always be in tune if you are soul mates.

8. **You feel secure and protected.** Regardless of the gender of your partner, he or she should always make you feel secure and protected. Your soul mate will make you feel like you have a guardian angel by your side. A person who plays on your insecurities, whether consciously or subconsciously, is not your soul mate.
9. **You can't imagine your life without him (or her).** A soul mate is not someone you can walk away from that easily. It is someone you can't imagine being without, a person you believe is worth sticking with and fighting for.
10. **You look each other in the eye.** Soul mates have a tendency to look into each other's eyes when speaking more often than ordinary couples. It comes naturally from the deep-seated connection between them. Looking a person in the eye when speaking denotes a high level of comfort and confidence.

Is the person you are considering as a mate someone who fits this criteria? If you already have a mate, does s/he fulfill this description of a soulmate? If not, you can work on developing the aspects of your relationship that are currently lacking. Show this list to your significant other. Have a frank discussion about what you feel is missing from your current relationship. Make a plan for developing these traits and habits.

Just remember, your mate has to want this as badly as you do, or your request will fall on deaf ears. Then you have a hard decision to make, move forward with the unfulfilling relationship you are in, or terminate the relationship and seek out your soulmate. Remember, you have worked too hard on developing your own mind, body and soul to allow another person to undermine your progress. If you and your mate are not negatively impacting one another's mind, body and soul development, then you will probably decide to stay, and perhaps you will find other activities to pursue that will help you feel fulfilled in life and continue in a relationship that is lukewarm. But if s/he is harming you physically, emotionally, mentally and/or spiritually you may decide to make an exit plan.

Soulmate...Where are you?

So where do you find the mate of your dreams? We have already discussed how to meditate on, and project for, the kind of mate that you want and need. This act alone will help you attract the kind of person you can love, respect, and value as a mate, but it doesn't guarantee that this person will magically appear on your doorstep. Envision yourself and your future mate doing things together that you both enjoy. Then get off the sofa, and go to that spot you saw in your vision.

A few years ago one of my single friends moved to a large city as part of an effort to reinvent herself. Although she was excited about embarking on her new life, she was also unsure about how to bring about the life she wanted. "I have no idea where to find someone to date," she confided. I suggested that we brainstorm some potential options for locating Mr. Right. "Are you politically involved," I asked. "I want to be," she responded. "Then join both local and national political movements and become active in your party," I suggested. "You will meet men with common passions and interests at every rally and meeting you attend." She also decided to join a local cycling club, and to volunteer at a local food bank. These were activities she wanted to pursue regardless of whether she found a mate while doing them or not. Not only did she end up having a ball, but Mr. Right, first located at a political rally, also turned out to be a bicyclist and a social justice advocate who volunteered at the homeless shelter. Talk about a match made in heaven!

Rediscover your Soulmate

You can rediscover your current mate in much the same way. Go on vacation, join a new group together, start a new venture that you have both always wanted to pursue. Be open to making some changes in yourself to accommodate your mate's preferences. Then ask your mate to be willing to do the same. If he is a stay-at-home guy find three new things to do together at home that you both enjoy; cooking, painting, remodeling, gardening, movie watching, working out; there are lots of new things you can do in an old place. Next, suggest that you try three things you would like to do outside the house; shopping, hiking, vacationing, going to a play, a protest march, a concert, a festival. If you add six new activities to your relationship it will immediately become more interesting. You will have more to talk about, more to look forward to together, and more good memories to reflect upon later. These are small things that can add up to a closer, more bonded, more rewarding relationship than you have at present.

Relationships, even those between soulmates, take one of three paths; they grow, stagnate or die. Even the best relationships can benefit from increased attention and effort. Relationships don't have to be sick in order to get better, so you need to work on yours on a continuous basis regardless of its current state of health. Pursuing new and interesting activities together energizes any relationship, but there is another strategy that is even more powerful in spurring mutual growth as a couple. Strive to become a better soulmate yourself! If you haven't met your soulmate yet you will have more luck attracting him/her if you become more like the person you are hoping to attract.

Be a Stellar Soulmate

On the chart below rate yourself on the characteristics that will make you a great soulmate. Place a checkmark next to the character traits that you feel you have mastered. Make a plan to develop up to five additional traits that you left unchecked.

✓	Character Traits
	Bearing-- the level to which something bad can be tolerated
	Confidence-- belief in oneself and one's powers or abilities
	Courage-- the quality of mind or spirit that enables a person to face difficulty, danger, pain
	Integrity-- adherence to moral and ethical principles; soundness of moral character
	Decisiveness-- firm or unwavering adherence to one's purpose
	Justice-- the practice of giving to others what is their due
	Endurance-- the ability or strength to continue or last
	Tact-- a keen sense of what to say or do to avoid giving offense
	Initiative-- an introductory act or step; leading action
	Coolness-- not excited; calm; composed; under control
	Maturity-- the ability to respond to the environment in an appropriate manner
	Improvement—bringing about a more valuable or desirable condition in yourself or your environment
	Will-- determined or sure
	Assertiveness—communicating an "I'm ok, you're ok" philosophy to others; communicating confidence
	Candor-- the quality of being open and honest in expression; frankness
	Sense of humor—appreciating and expressing the funny aspect of a situation
	Competence-- the ability to do something successfully or efficiently
	Commitment-- the state or quality of being dedicated to a cause
	Creativity-- the use of the imagination or original ideas
	Self-discipline-- the ability to control one's feelings and overcome one's weaknesses; the ability to pursue what one thinks is right despite temptations to abandon it

	Humility-- a modest or low view of one's own importance; humbleness
	Flexibility-- the quality of bending easily without breaking
	Empathy/Compassion-- the ability to understand and share the feelings of another; concern for the sufferings or misfortunes of others

Traits Targeted for Development	What will you do to develop this trait in yourself?
1.	
2.	
3.	
4.	
5.	

Character traits are not easy to develop. If they were everyone would be of high character and then we would not have a world full of hatred, wars, bigotry and greed. Becoming a person of high character is well worth the time you invest in improving yourself in this area, and those around you, you soulmate, your friends, coworkers, and family will benefit as much as you do from your evolving consciousness.

Building character is an ongoing task. You will probably never be entirely satisfied with the character traits you possess. That is okay. Focusing on becoming a better, more mature, more compassionate person is about the journey, not the destination. The journey is what you are involved in at present, and presents a new start point for you each day. It is about making every day better than the day before for yourself and those around you. And then you will begin to discover true magic. When you improve so will your soulmate. There will be less fighting, because you will not engage, and your soulmate will begin to notice that they are less stressed when they encounter less disagreement from you.

Now wait a minute! Why should you have to do all the growing? Shouldn't your soulmate have to evolve into a better person too? Of course! But you are participating in this program, and s/he isn't. Ideally you would work through this book together, but realistically that almost never happens. When you recommend this approach to your soulmate, s/he will perceive it as you trying to "fix" him/her and will resist. It is always more effective to model the behavior you wish to see from your mate rather than to request, or worse yet, demand it. Remember that your female brain is perfectly designed to be a role model, and to hear the messages the soul sends you to guide your thinking and behavior. But male brains aren't structured the same way. Their brains are designed to support the "hunter" role in nature, while women are designed to be gatherers. When men hunt, it is a single-minded activity. They wait for their prey, find it and kill it. It is an entirely task-focused activity that uses primarily the left brain.

Women's brains are structured to support relationship-focused perspectives. We care as much about the impact we are having on others as we do about their impact on us. In prehistoric times men were tasked to hunt for the survival of their species, and women were responsible for gathering edible vegetation and fruits. Women gathered in groups, singing, talking and tending to children while picking berries or digging roots. Female brains had to accommodate multi-tasking, while male brains evolved in a more linear fashion.

Yet today, women are the real relationship experts, while men are proficient at "getting the job done." In short, it is a woman's job to mentor a man in the more subtle aspects of a relationship. Since men live in a "show me" world, if you wish a man to evolve you must demonstrate the evolution you desire. If you want him to be gentler, you become gentler to him. If you want him to be more heroic, show him some heroism. If you study men closely you will find that this is the strategy they use to improve one another. They master a task, show another guy what they did, and then dare him to do better. It is called "oneupsmanship" and men do it in sports, the military, at work and at home. Show him what you can do. He will probably accept the challenge.

A Real Woman

Janna knew that Jonathan was her soulmate since shortly after she met him. They shared the same "offbeat" sense of humor, had learned similar lessons from their life experiences, and reacted with one mind to the events that were unfolding in their daily lives. Yes, they both felt as though previous to meeting, each of them was "half" and had now become "whole." This was not to say that each of them couldn't function independently, they could. Both were busy professionals who had to travel separately for work, but their time together was pure harmony, something neither of them had experienced in their past relationships.

Now, celebrating their eighth anniversary, things were different. Rather than facing the challenges of the world together they were doing it separately. Even though they were sitting in a romantic restaurant enjoying candlelight and champagne, they weren't really together. Each lost in their own thoughts, they only occasionally focused on one another, and even then, the moment of shared attention was fleeting and superficial. Although she was concerned about the ever growing distance she felt from Jonathan, Janna didn't know quite what to do about it. She yearned for the days when they went to sleep cuddling each evening rather than nodding off while watching TV as occurred now. The last time she invited Jon to cuddle he had told her quite sternly that he had no time to cuddle. He needed to get his fantasy football picks done.

As a matter of fact Jonathan was usually short with her these days, and much of their interaction left Janna feeling as though she was simply an irritation to him. Out of hurt and frustration Janna had begun to withdraw, seldom initiating any conversation with her soulmate, out of fear that he would treat her ideas with disregard, or even disrespect. Neither did it help that Jonathan had a new protégé at work who seemed to impress him at every turn. He had even begun quoting her to Janna and had suggested several times that she could benefit from being more like the young woman.

Janna entertained a number of ideas as to how to proceed. There was a guy at work that had been flirty lately, and she could give him some play. Or she could just decide that she didn't care about the quality of her relationship with Jonathan and adapt to a life of disconnection and disinterest. That was certainly easier than leaving the relationship, or vying for attention with someone she didn't even know.

While cleaning out her desk one day she came across a card that Jonathan had given her on their first anniversary. She remembered finding the card beside her on her pillow upon awakening that day. Warm memories of that morning flooded her being. In that moment, as her soul spoke loudly to her, Janna knew that she wanted that feeling back again. That evening Janna had the first anniversary card waiting for Jonathan when he arrived home. The note inside expressed her unwavering love for him and bore a list of things that she wanted to thank him for. It ended with an invitation to have a meaningful conversation about their mutual goals and future plans.

For the first time in over a year Jonathan's face softened when he read the note. He hugged Janna tightly and spoke softly. "Thank you Janna," he said. "We have always stood by each other, but we seem to be standing acres apart lately." She saw the fatigue in his face, and perceived it in her own as well. "I think it's time to lean on each other a bit more," she offered. "I know I have become too busy to laugh with you, and I have a strong need to be an expert on everything, so I know I am right about this!"

"For once I'll agree with your wisdom without putting up a fight," Jonathan grinned. Soulmates can rediscover each other...again and again.

The Stress Mess

"One of the most calming and powerful actions you can do to intervene in a stormy world is to stand up and show your soul. Struggling souls catch light from other souls who are fully lit and willing to show it." Dr. Clarissa Pinkola Estés

Recently I queried my Facebook friends as to what made them feel the most stressed and the least confident. A dozen friends responded immediately, three men and nine women. The names I have given them are aliases to protect their identities. The men gave the following answers;

- Jack: Money! The most stressful thing for me is making sure that I have enough money to provide for my family.
- Don: People who are supposed to be your friends and are so judgmental of everything.
- Phil: Assholes!

The women replied;

- Renee: Evidently, although I didn't feel it, my husband being away all the time working has me stressed out to the point where I got hives so bad I had to go to the doctor. Stress is any negative feeling we carry, sometimes even when we don't realize what harm it is doing to us. I don't feel confident when I think about aging, becoming more dependent on others.
- Danita: The death of a loved one.
- Kathy: Taking an older person to the doctor and watching them being treated as if their age is the only thing wrong with them.
- Shannon: I am a pleaser!! I want to make everything alright...it could be family, friends, work or even a stranger and when I see someone hurting, not having enough money, etc. I wish I could fix it!! Just wish people could be happy and have what they need!
- Connie: When I haven't prepared enough or early enough.
- Marilyn: The health of my children. I am raising a child with mental illness in a culture that continues to demean and stigmatize mental illness.
- Megan: What stresses me is not having affordable health care options. I feel least confident when I am wearing my old clothes because I can't afford to buy new ones.
- April: Money stresses me out.
- Sami: What makes me feel stressed is my kids are struggling in life and always think that they can come to me to bail them out. What makes me lack confident is the fact that I didn't teach them how to be independent and self-sufficient and that they will never get it right.

Wow, that is a ton of trouble from just a dozen people! The lesser world is full of stress, and much of it is beyond our control. And it never stops! Danita, who was adjusting to the death of her husband when she responded to my post, last month lost her 35-year-old daughter who died unexpectedly in her sleep. Despite putting on a brave face, it is clear that she is grieving her losses daily.

Sami has been a kind and loving mom for the 25 years that I have known her, yet her adult children bring her more problems than anyone could reasonably expect. Since her posting she has been blessed with two new infant granddaughters who are the light of her life, but the new babies are not helping with the self-sufficiency goals she has for their parents.

Renee is a self-confident professional woman who is always there with reassurance and advocacy for others when they need her. Her husband finally returned from working abroad and was home for less than a month when he had a heart attack. He spent two weeks on a ventilator and began breathing on his own again recently. Renee is recovering from a prolonged attack of hives.

Shannon is someone I have known since kindergarten. She was a "pleaser" then too, and the most pleasant person you will ever meet. Connie owns a thriving consulting firm, and Marilyn is a fierce advocate for justice and fairness for all. Stress does not discriminate. No matter your calling, your income, your confidence level, or your gender. Your life will be burdened by stress on a continuous basis.

Stress Can Make You Sick

Have you ever heard of "psychosomatic illness?" It is a condition that occurs when your mind makes your body sick. A process known as "General Adaptation Syndrome" explains how this happens.

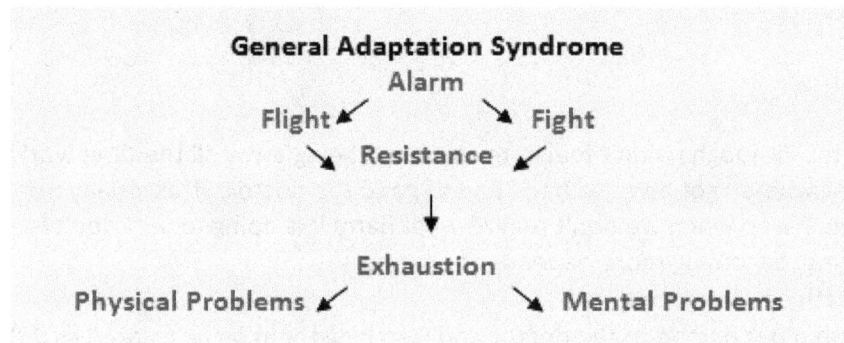

General Adaptation Syndrome
Alarm
Flight   Fight
Resistance
↓
Exhaustion
Physical Problems   Mental Problems

When something stressful happens to you it creates a sensation of "alarm." The more intense the stressor, the more alarm you feel. Sometimes it is so severe it makes your chest tighten and you can't find your voice or catch your breath for a second. At that moment your body produces a big dose of adrenaline (Cortisol) to prepare you for "flight or fight." This worked fine for prehistoric man who had to wrestle saber-toothed tigers but it isn't nearly as effective with the problems reported by my Facebook friends. Running away, or donning boxing gloves just isn't a practical way to resolve issues involving family, money, friends and social ills. The adrenaline doesn't get burned away by a physically strenuous activity so it just causes your blood pressure to go up, your pulse to quicken, your digestive system to start secreting stomach acid, and your muscles to tense and ache.

Even more disturbing is the fact that your brain can't tell the difference between a real and perceived event. Every time you think about or talk about the stressor that is causing you to feel alarmed your body will think the event is happening again, and will give you another spurt of adrenaline to deal with it. Over time, your adrenaline levels will just stay high, causing you to become exhausted due to the fact that your body is working overtime in response to what your mind is telling it. Exhaustion leads to illness of one sort or another. You might become chronically depressed or anxious, or you might develop a "psychosomatic" illness such as high blood pressure, blood sugar elevation in diabetics, muscular pain, especially in the head, neck and back, insomnia, lowered resistance to colds and flu, heart disease, and a host of other serious illnesses.

When I was a mental health nurse one of the first assessments I would administer to a new client was a psychosocial stressor scale known as Holmes and Rahe Stress Scale. It is a well validated test that is able to tell you if you are at risk of becoming ill due to the current stress in your life. Let's see how you come out. To measure stress according to the Holmes and Rahe Stress Scale, the number of "Life Change Units" that apply to events in the past year of an individual's life are added and the final score will give a rough estimate of how stress affects health. List your score in the third column, then total your score.

Life event	Life change units	Your Score
Death of a spouse/significant other	100	
Divorce	73	
Marital separation	65	
Imprisonment	63	
Death of a close family member	63	
Personal injury or illness	53	
Marriage	50	
Dismissal from work	47	
Marital reconciliation	45	
Retirement	45	
Change in health of family member	44	
Pregnancy	40	
Sexual difficulties	39	
Gain a new family member	39	
Business readjustment	39	
Change in financial state	38	
Death of a close friend	37	
Change to different line of work	36	
Change in frequency of arguments	35	
Major mortgage	32	
Foreclosure of mortgage or loan	30	
Change in responsibilities at work	29	
Child leaving home	29	
Trouble with in-laws	29	
Outstanding personal achievement	28	
Spouse starts or stops work	26	
Beginning or end school	26	
Change in living conditions	25	
Revision of personal habits	24	
Trouble with boss	23	
Change in working hours or conditions	20	
Change in residence	20	
Change in schools	20	
Change in recreation	19	
Change in church activities	19	
Change in social activities	18	
Minor mortgage or loan	17	
Change in sleeping habits	16	
Change in number of family reunions	15	
Change in eating habits	15	
Vacation	13	
Christmas	12	
Minor violation of law	11	
	Your Total Score	

Score of 300+: At risk of illness.
Score of 150-299: Risk of illness is moderate (reduced by 30% from the above risk).
Score <150: Only a slight risk of illness.

Are you at risk to become ill due to the cumulative stressors in your life? If so, let's discuss how to rid yourself of the stress that accompanies various life events.

Renee and Danita have little chance to recover from their stressors in the immediate future because the hits just keep on coming. The moment they felt a bit of relief from their original stressors a related occurrence propelled them into even greater amounts of stress. The death of a spouse or family member and the changing health of a family member are very high on the scale. Given the cumulative impact of Danita's husband and daughter dying in the same year, and Renee's husband's illness on the heels of returning home have plunged these women into situations that they could not anticipate, control or repair. Their attention must focus on caring for themselves in order to stay healthy until the pressure of their current worries begin to subside.

Shannon and Connie have a much better chance of resolving the stress in their lives because their issues are under their own control. Connie can strive to organize herself to become more timely and efficient in doing her work. Shannon can rethink her need to please everyone, and can begin reining in her need to please by deciding that she must please herself first, and then attend to the needs and wants of others.

In short, you begin to reduce the stress in your life by taking charge of the things you have control over and the ability and willingness to change. Even during unexpectedly tough times you can maintain your health and sanity if you can hold smaller stressors in your life at bay. Please take a few minutes and analyze the major stressors in your life over the past five years.

Analyze Your Stress Reactions

If you keep an appointment book, journal or diary please retrieve those documents dated over the last five years. Begin by reading what you wrote about your life over the past five years. Even if you are just reviewing your business appointments from five years ago the memories will come flooding back and you will be reminded of the stressors you experienced during that year of your life. Fill out the following table based on your recollections.

Years	Top 3 Stessors	Resolved or ongoing?	How resolved? Why ongoing?
5 years ago…			
4 years ago…			
3 years ago…			
2 years ago…			
Last year…			

Take a close look at the results of your analysis. Is there a pattern? Do the same stressors keep cropping up in your life again and again? Are there some stressors that you are more effective in addressing than others? What is keeping you from addressing recurring or ongoing stressors in a manner that reduces or resolves them? Did you grow stronger from addressing your stressors, or did they cause you to regress or break down? Did you prevail over your stress more often than it conquered you?

You have now taken the first step in reducing the stress in your life. As you examined your stressors you probably noticed that most stressors in your life have dissipated once a given situation was over. If you can keep major stressors from making you sick as they are occurring, the battle is half won.

During any time of crisis it is extremely important to take care of yourself to at least the same extent that you are taking care of others. Rest, eat, exercise, meditate and take some time to laugh, read a book or watch a movie. Get out of your own head to give yourself a respite from living in fight-or-flight mode.

> I've only just realised how utterly exhausted and drained I am after living in a near constant state of fight-or-flight for so long.

Send yourself positive affirmations, "This too shall pass," is usually true and can be quite comforting when you don't think you can take another moment of the trauma and drama you are facing. "What doesn't kill you makes you stronger," is another empowering affirmation you can use to remind yourself that you will be a better person as a result of what you are facing. Notice the new learning, personal growth, and new perspectives you gain as you go through a stressful situation. Be aware of the good decisions you are making to handle the situation in the best way possible. Give yourself permission to feel good about yourself even if the stress you are dealing with is of your own making.

Let go of the stress after the situation is over. Do not allow yourself to wallow in self-defeating thoughts. Once you have done all you can in a stressful situation, and the situation has improved, move on! Don't cling to the "should haves" or "would haves" that are residual in your mind. You did your best, and your best was good enough to get you through the situation. Consider having a "letting go" ceremony. Burn any non-essential documents involved with the situation, take the gifts that the person you are at odds with gave you and donate them to charity, write a goodbye letter and then shred the letter use it as confetti! Do whatever you need to do to leave the stress in your past.

But sometimes the situation won't let you move on. Let's say your big stressor is an obnoxious ex-husband who caused you to struggle through a long and ugly divorce several years ago He may still be causing you problems with ongoing custody or child support battles. If so, see each episode of stress as a new chapter in the continuing saga rather than one long fight. Savor your victories; your divorce was finalized, you still have custody of the kids, and he does pay child support on occasion. Noting your progress will give you the energy and positive attitude you need for the next round of craziness that your ex-husband is sure to bring you. Nothing succeeds like success, so count your successes. They will calm you and give you the confidence you need to preserve.

Another strategy that works well to address ongoing stressors is to change your mind about what you want or expect from the situation. If your ex-husband is unreliable about paying child support you can decide that you would rather not take his money anyway, or you could suggest that his support payment be lowered so it will be easier for him to pay. Remember not to let your anger or frustration to dictate your response to a given situation. Sometimes it makes more sense to switch than fight, or to accept the reality of a situation rather than to continue hoping against hope that things will change in a way that is more favorable to you.

I recently spoke with an elderly man who was suffering from a number of physical ailments that were made worse by a major stressor in his life. After the passing of his wife his step-daughter made off with the family fortune along with all of her mother's belongings. After consulting several attorneys he learned that even after a protracted court fight he would only end up with about $10,000 from his wife's estate. "Let's brainstorm five ways to get $10,000 that would be easier than fighting for it in court," I suggested. Ten minutes later we had listed eight ways he could acquire an extra $10,000 without going through the stress of a court hearing. He decided to stop fighting for money, and his health improved almost immediately.

Look at your stress analysis again. Is there an ongoing or recurring stressor in your life that you could resolve permanently if you changed your thinking or behavior in the situation? Below list any recurring stressors that you have yet to resolve. Under each one brainstorm at least three ways that you could change your thinking or behavior to bring the situation to a permanent end.

Recurring stressor:
Possible change:
Possible change:
Possible change:

Find the ideas you listed that hold the most appeal for you, and begin doing the new behavior or using your new thinking immediately. You will look better, feel better and be better once the albatross you have been carrying around is no longer hanging from your neck.

Along with the major stressors in your life there are also a myriad of smaller stressors that occur to you daily. Here is where another affirmation might help to bring daily irritants into perspective, "Don't sweat the small stuff." Fortunately, most of it is small stuff. People make mistakes, or misunderstand you, or don't listen, or don't agree with you. It happens. Let go of it in real time. Understand that you have bigger fish to fry, and that if you allow yourself to suffer in the face of small things you are in essence giving your power, your peace and your attention over to things that are insignificant in the long run. Just say no to stressing over small things. They just aren't worth ruining your day or your health over.

Compliments of Reader's Digest, here are 37 tips to relieve your stress. Try one or more daily to relieve both large and small stressors in your life.

Stress Management Tips

1. Breathe Easily
"Breathing from your diaphragm oxygenates your blood, which helps you relax almost instantly," says Robert Cooper, Ph.D., the San Francisco coauthor of *The Power of 5* (Rodale Press, 1996), a book of five-second and five-minute health tips. Shallow chest breathing, by contrast, can cause your heart to beat faster and your muscles to tense up, exacerbating feelings of stress. To breathe deeply, begin by putting your hand on your abdomen just below the navel. Inhale slowly through your nose and watch your hand move out as your belly expands. Hold the breath for a few seconds, then exhale slowly. Repeat several times.

2. Visualize Calm
It sounds New Age-y, but at least one study, done at the Cleveland Clinic Foundation, has found that it's highly effective in reducing stress. Dr. Cooper recommends imagining you're in a hot shower and a wave of relaxation is washing your stress down the drain. Gerald Epstein, M.D., the New York City author of *Healing Visualizations* (Bantam Doubleday Dell Press, 1989), suggests the following routine: Close your eyes, take three long, slow breaths, and spend a few seconds picturing a relaxing scene, such as walking in a meadow, kneeling by a brook, or lying on the beach. Focus on the details—the sights, the sounds, the smells.

3. Make Time for a Mini Self-Massage
Maria Hernandez-Reif, Ph.D., of the Touch Research Institute at the University of Miami School of Medicine, recommends simply massaging the palm of one hand by making a circular motion with the thumb of the other. Or use a massage gadget. The SelfCare catalog offers several, such as the S-shaped Tamm unit, that allow you to massage hard-to-reach spots on your back. For a free catalog, call 800-345-3371 or go to www.selfcare.com.

4. Try a Tonic
A study at Duke University in Durham, NC, found homeopathy effective in quelling anxiety disorders. Look for stress formulas such as Nerve Tonic (from Hyland) or Sedalia (from Boiron) in your health food store, or consult

a licensed homeopath. To find one near you, contact the National Center for Homeopathy, 801 North Fairfax St., Suite 306, Alexandria, VA 22314; 703-548-7790 or go to www.healthy.net.

5. Say Cheese

Smiling is a two-way mechanism. We do it when we're relaxed and happy, but doing it can also make us feel relaxed and happy. "Smiling transmits nerve impulses from the facial muscles to the limbic system, a key emotional center in the brain, tilting the neurochemical balance toward calm," Dr. Cooper explains. Go ahead and grin. Don't you feel better already?

6. Do Some Math

Using a scale of one to 10, with one being the equivalent of a minor hassle and 10 being a true catastrophe, assign a number to whatever it is that's making you feel anxious. "You'll find that most problems we encounter rate somewhere in the two to five range—in other words, they're really not such a big deal," says Dr. Elkin.

7. Stop Gritting Your Teeth

Stress tends to settle in certain parts of our bodies, the jaw being one of them. When things get hectic, try this tip from Dr. Cooper: Place your index fingertips on your jaw joints, just in front of your ears; clench your teeth and inhale deeply. Hold the breath for a moment, and as you exhale say, "Ah-h-h-h," then unclench your teeth. Repeat a few times.

8. Compose a Mantra

Devise an affirmation — a short, clear, positive statement that focuses on your coping abilities. "Affirmations are a good way to silence the self-critical voice we all carry with us that only adds to our stress," Dr. Elkin says. The next time you feel as if your life is one disaster after another, repeat 10 times, "I feel calm. I can handle this."

9. Check Your Chi

Qigong (pronounced chee-gong) is a 5,000-year-old Chinese practice designed to promote the flow of chi, the vital life force that flows throughout the body, regulating its functions. Qigong master Ching-Tse Lee, Ph.D., a professor of psychology at Brooklyn College in New York, recommends this calming exercise: Stand with your feet shoulder-width apart and parallel. Bend your knees to a quarter-squat position (about 45 degrees) while keeping your upper body straight. Observe your breathing for a couple of breaths. Inhale and bring your arms slowly up in front of you to shoulder height with your elbows slightly bent. Exhale, stretching your arms straight out. Inhale again, bend your elbows slightly and drop your arms down slowly until your thumbs touch the sides of your legs. Exhale one more time, then stand up straight.

10. Be a Fighter

"At the first sign of stress, you often hear people complain, 'What did I do to deserve this?'" says Dr. Cooper. The trouble is, feeling like a victim only increases feelings of stress and helplessness. Instead, focus on being proactive. If your flight gets canceled, don't wallow in self-pity. Find another one. If your office is too hot or too cold, don't suffer in silence. Call the building manager and ask what can be done to make things more comfortable.

11. Put It on Paper

Writing provides perspective, says Paul J. Rosch, M.D., president of the American Institute of Stress in Yonkers, NY. Divide a piece of paper into two parts. On the left side, list the stressors you may be able to change, and on the right, list the ones you can't. "Change what you can," Dr. Rosch suggests, "and stop fretting over what you can't."

12. Count to 10

Before you say or do something you'll regret, step away from the stressor and collect yourself, advises Dr. Cooper. You can also look away for a moment or put the caller on hold. Use your time-out to take a few deep breaths, stretch, or recite an affirmation.

13. Switch to Decaf

Wean yourself slowly, or you might get a caffeine-withdrawal headache that could last for several days, cautions James Duke, Ph.D., the Fulton, MD, author of *The Green Pharmacy* (Rodale Press, 1997). Subtract a little regular coffee and add some decaf to your morning cup. Over the next couple of weeks, gradually increase the proportion of decaf to regular until you're drinking all decaf. You should also consider switching from regular soft drinks to caffeine-free ones or sparkling mineral water.

14. Just Say No
Trying to do everything is a one-way ticket to serious stress. Be clear about your limits, and stop trying to please everyone all the time.

15. Take a Whiff
Oils of anise, basil, bay, chamomile, eucalyptus, lavender, peppermint, rose, and thyme are all soothing, say Kathy Keville and Mindy Green, coauthors of *Aromatherapy: A Complete Guide to the Healing Art* (Crossing Press, 1995). Place a few pieces of rock salt in a small vial, then add a couple of drops of the oil of your choice (the rock salt absorbs the oil and is much less risky to carry around in your purse than a bottle of oil). Open the vial and breathe in the scent whenever you need a quick stress release. Look for the oils in your local health food store, or online.

16. Warm Up
Try this tip from David Sobel, M.D., in San Jose, CA, author of The Healthy Mind, Healthy Body Handbook (I S H K Book Service, 1997). Rub your hands together vigorously until they feel warm. Then cup them over your closed eyes for five seconds while you breathe deeply. The warmth and darkness are comforting.

17. Say Yes to Pressure
Acupressure stimulates the same points as acupuncture, but with fingers instead of needles. Michael Reed Gach, Ph.D., director of the Acupressure Institute in Berkeley, CA, recommends pressing on the following three points:

- The Third Eye, located between the eyebrows, in the indentation where the bridge of the nose meets the forehead.
- The Heavenly Pillar, on the back of the neck slightly below the base of the skull, about half an inch to the left or right of the spine.
- The Heavenly Rejuvenation, half an inch below the top of each shoulder, midway between the base of the neck and the outside of the shoulder blade.
- Breathe deeply and apply firm, steady pressure on each point for two to three minutes. The pressure should cause a mild aching sensation, but not pain.

18. Schedule Worry Time
Some stressors demand immediate attention — a smoke alarm siren or a police car's whirling red light. But many low-grade stressors can be dealt with at a later time, when it's more convenient. "File them away in a little mental compartment, or make a note," Dr. Elkin says, "then deal with them when the time is right. Don't let them control you."

19. Shake It Up
This quick exercise helps loosen the muscles in your neck and upper back, says Dr. Sobel: Stand or sit, stretch your arms out from your sides and shake your hands vigorously for about 10 seconds. Combine this with a little deep breathing, Dr. Sobel says, and you'll do yourself twice as much good.

20. Munch Some Snacks
Foods that are high in carbohydrates stimulate the release of serotonin, feel-good brain chemicals that help induce calm, says Dr. Cooper. Crackers, pretzels, or a bagel should do the trick.

21. Boost Your Vitamin Intake
Elizabeth Somer, R.D., author of *Food and Mood* (Owl Books, 1999), in Salem, OR, recommends that women take a daily multivitamin and mineral formula that contains between 100% and 300% of the recommended dietary allowances of vitamin B, as well as the minerals calcium, magnesium, chromium, copper, iron, manganese, molybdenum, selenium and zinc. Avoid stress formulas, which often contain large amounts of randomly formulated nutrients, such as the B vitamins, but little or nothing else, Somer says.

22. Get Horizontal
If sex has been on the bottom of your to-do list for too long, move it to the top. Sex increases levels of endorphins, those mood-boosting chemicals in the brain, and it's one of the best total-body relaxers around,

says Louanne Cole Weston, Ph.D., a sex therapist in Sacramento, CA. Make a date with your mate, and don't let anything get in the way.

23. Admit It
Each of us has uniquely individual stress signals — neck or shoulder pain, shallow breathing, stammering, teeth gritting, queasiness, loss of temper. Learn to identify yours, then say out loud, "I'm feeling stressed," when they crop up, recommends Dr. Rosch. Recognizing your personal stress signals helps slow the buildup of negativity and anxiety.

24. Space Out
Look out the window and find something natural that captures your imagination, advises Dr. Sobel. Notice the clouds rolling by or the wind in the trees.

25. Try Tea
By now most of us know about the calming properties of chamomile tea. But a steaming cup of catnip, passionflower, skullcap or kava kava also work, according to Dr. Duke. Whether you use tea bags or loose tea (one teaspoon of tea per cup of boiling water), steep for about 10 minutes to get the full benefits of the herbs.

26. Take a Walk
It forces you to breathe more deeply and improves circulation, says Dr. Cooper. Step outside if you can; if that's not possible, you can gain many of the same benefits simply by walking to the bathroom or water cooler, or by pacing back and forth. "The key is to get up and move," Dr. Cooper says.

27. Soak it Up
"When I have the time, nothing is more stress relieving for me than a hot bath," Dr. Weston says. "But when I don't have time, I do the next-best thing: I wash my face or even just my hands and arms with hot water. The key is to imagine that I'm taking a hot bath. It's basically a visualization exercise, but the hot water makes it feel real."

28. Play a Few Bars
A number of recent studies have shown that music can do everything from slow heart rate to increase endorphins. Good bets: Bach's "Air on the G-String," Beethoven's *Pastorale* symphony, Chopin's Nocturne in G, Handel's *Water Music,* or pianist George Winston's CDs *Autumn* or *December.*.

29. Fall for Puppy Love
In a study of 100 women conducted last year at the State University of New York at Buffalo, researchers found that those who owned a dog had lower blood pressure than those who didn't. If you don't have a pooch, visit a friend's: Petting an animal for just a couple of minutes helps relieve stress, researchers have found.

30. Practice Mindfulness
Heighten your awareness of the moment by focusing intently on an object. Notice a pencil's shape, color, weight and feel. Or slowly savor a raisin or a piece of chocolate. Mindfulness leads to relaxation.

31. Dial a Friend
Sharing your troubles can give you perspective, help you feel cared for and relieve your burden.

32. Stretch
Muscles tighten during the course of the day, and when we feel stressed out, the process accelerates. Stretching loosens muscles and encourages deep breathing. Molly Fox, creative fitness director at the Equinox Fitness Center in New York City, says one of the greatest stress-relieving stretches is a yoga position called the child pose, which stretches the back muscles. On a rug or mat, kneel, sit back on your heels, then lean forward and put your forehead on the floor and your arms alongside your legs, palms up. Hold for one to three minutes.

33. Say a Little Prayer
Studies show that compared with those who profess no faith, religious and spiritual people are calmer and healthier.

34. Make Plans
"Looking forward to something provides calming perspective," Dr. Elkin says. Buy concert tickets, schedule a weekend getaway, or make an appointment for a massage.

35. Goof Off

It temporarily removes you from a potentially stressful situations. Esther Orioli, president of Essi Systems, a San Francisco consultant company that organizes stress-management programs, keeps a harmonica in the drawer for when she's feeling stressed out. Bonus: Playing it promotes deep breathing.

36. Straighten Up

When people are under stress, they slump over as if they have the weight of the world on their shoulders. "Slumping restricts breathing and reduces blood and oxygen flow to the brain, adding to muscle tension and magnifying feelings of panic and helplessness," Dr. Cooper explains. Straightening your spine has just the opposite effect. It promotes circulation, increases oxygen levels in your blood and helps lessen muscle tension, all of which promote relaxation.

37. Tiptoe Through the Tulips

Tending your garden helps get you out of your head and lets you commune with nature, a known stress reliever. If you're not a gardener, tend to a houseplant. Plants = growth = cycle of life, a nice reminder that stress, too, will pass.

A Real Woman

It only took six months for Ella to realize that retirement wasn't the paradise that she thought it would be. After losing her husband last year it had become harder and harder to leave the house each day, and to go to a job where they clearly perceived her as a dinosaur. The job had become so bureaucratic that it was nearly impossible to attend to the real purpose of the work, helping unwed mothers finish their education, and her new supervisor showed no interest for her concerns. When management offered a buy-out to tenured workers Ella jumped at the chance to retire, even if it meant losing 25% of her pension.

At first retirement was fine. Ella cleaned her house and got rid of years of accumulated junk, signed on to Facebook for the first time ever, and found a number of high school friends that she had lost contract with through the years, and even took a couple of day trips with a local seniors group. But lately she felt sad and listless most of the time, and she ached from head to toe. The doctor diagnosed her as having chronic fatigue syndrome, but Ella knew the truth. She was tired of life. No one would even miss her if she died today. Come to think of it, dying wouldn't be a bad idea, because her money wasn't going to hold out much longer anyway.

Throughout her career Ella had fantasized that her golden years would be her best years. She envisioned herself and her husband taking lavish vacations, pursuing their hobbies, and cuddling cute grandchildren. But hubby was gone, leaving her large medical bills and no life insurance money, her son was gay and living in Europe, and her hobbies held no interest for her anymore. Ella stopped Facebooking, seldom bothered to get dressed, and found herself lying down most of the time.

Then came the call that she almost didn't answer. It was her former manager and the woman was in a real pickle. Two new staffers had resigned, no one had written the annual grant needed to fund the program, and they failed the latest audit from the state. Would it be possible for Ella to come back to work part-time, at half of her former salary on a one-month contract to get things back on track?

Ella's first reaction was to laugh and hang up, but she told the manager that she would consider the offer, and get back to her in a few days. Her head was spinning as Ella considered her answer. Although retirement was not a dream come true, at least it wasn't the hell that work had been. And how was she to straighten out eight months of neglect and errors in a month, part-time, with her rude coworkers complaining that she was "double-dipping" and being overpaid? She couldn't and she wouldn't she suddenly realized.

Over the next two days Ella drafted a counter-offer to consult at her former job for a period of six months at twice the salary she once made. She devised a work plan to show what she would accomplish during the term of her contract, and she proposed a change in methodology that would improve program results and give meaningful help to their young clientele. Her hands shook as she pushed the send button on the email.

As she waited for a response to her proposal Ella felt fully alive for the first time in months. Miraculously she barely ached at all, and didn't feel tired for a change. No, she felt excited. Not only could she consult for her former employer, but she could begin offering similar to services to other area non-profits. She was still one of the best grant writers in the area, and she possessed a host of skills that would be of value to other social service agencies.

When the manager finally called to negotiate a contract with her Ella was so busy setting up her corporation and building her website that she was again tempted to ignore the call. But in the end she prevailed and was able to return to her former job with renewed enthusiasm for the work. No one disrespected her now, they were grateful for her help, and even allowed her to teach them her methods and philosophies.

Two years after starting her consulting firm Ella had expanded to doing national and international work. She now travels to places she has always wanted to visit, and even got to spend time with her son when she was awarded a European contract.

No, life didn't turn out exactly as Ella had hoped, but it was better than she could have ever imagined. Once she stopped feeling sorry for herself, and made peace with the fact that her dreams were not to be realized she began to generate new dreams, better dreams, dreams that put her in control of her own life. She is now a happy, productive professional who swears that she will never retire. She doesn't want to die anymore, but if she must, she wants to die on the job!

Conflict, Kids and Courage

"Courage is what it takes to stand up and speak; courage is also what it takes to sit down and listen." Winston Churchill

I noticed two glaring omissions from the Holmes and Rahe Stress Scale presented in the last chapter. There is no direct reference to being in a conflict, which is something many women find quite stressful, and there were few statements that related to being a parent. The birth of a child, and the child leaving home are noted on the scale, but these two events, at least for me, were much less stressful than everything that happened between those two events.

In this chapter we will discuss both conflict management and parenting since they tend to go hand in hand, and we will talk a bit about how to cultivate courage, a handy character trait to have if you are to parent children or resolve conflict.

I have never met a mother who isn't worried about her children. It matters little whether they are babies, teens or middle-aged adults, universally and persistently mothers worry about their off-spring from their birth to the grave. They also tend to blame themselves for whatever failures manifest in their children's lives, and others blame them as well. Ask almost any mother about the most difficult role they have ever fulfilled, and she will tell you that it is being a "good" parent.

The problem is that there is no clear definition of "good parent." Yes, we all know we are to be loving and supportive as parents, and we are to use "tough" love when our children resist any other kind of love we might offer, but there is no specific recipe for success. Every book written on parenting recommends a different approach to raising happy, healthy, productive kids. In the final analysis parenting turns out to be a crap shoot. You put the best you have into it and hope it is enough of the right stuff to contribute to the healthy holistic development of your precious babies.

Regardless of how good we are as moms, we will not raise perfect children because there is no such thing. Yet, that is the exact aim of most mothers. Striving to attain the impossible is always stressful add to the fact that the very nature of parenting requires us to push other humans in a direction that they typically don't want to follow, and it is little wonder that mothers don't become quite insane long before their little ones are grown.

Although parenthood carries with it more rewards than any other job on the planet, it is also the most challenging. Perhaps the most challenging part is that your children know you as well as you know them. They can predict your reactions and know how to manipulate you based on both your strengths and weaknesses. But you love them more than you ever knew you could love anyone, so you stay invested in giving your very best to them.

Mothers ask me for advice about their kids on a regular basis. I hear about children who are failing in school, taking drugs, hanging with the wrong crowd, being rebellious, or are overly spoiled. They all love their children and mostly blame themselves, their co-parent, or their extended family for the problems their children are facing. Few blame the children themselves whether they are still small, or are fully grown adult offspring. I share my views on childrearing with them in spiritual terms as I am about to share them with you. I am neither entitled nor qualified to tell someone else how to raise their children, but I do hope to offer some nontraditional perspectives that might provide a broader view of parenthood than is generally discussed.

I Never Asked to Be Born!

At some point in a child's life they usually feel compelled to tell their parents that they are sad to be associated with them. This information might come with the declaration, "I never asked to be born." Well, maybe so and maybe no. Early in our relationship my husband introduced me to a set of spiritual studies that support the theory of reincarnation. Our studies have informed us that it takes several incarnations to learn the lessons that humans need to know to master love and become more God-like. That is where the concept of "old souls" comes from. Some children come into the world with a level of wisdom that cannot be explained in terms of their age or earthly experiences. These are souls re-entering the world, some for the final time before residing permanently in the cosmic consciousness to be masters who guide us through soul communications. Some might call them angels, but in our spiritual teachings we refer to them as Masters.

We believe that we travel from one lifetime to another with our soul group, a core group of individual souls who are brought together to teach and learn from one another in an effort to evolve towards being fully loving beings, like God. We are taught that the human lifecycle is approximately 144 years in length with humans spending about half their time in earth school and the other half as spiritual beings. During the second half of our lifecycle we reflect on what we have learned in our last incarnation and what we might yet need to learn in the next one. Once we settle on the lessons that need to come our way we choose the situation in which we will begin our next life cycle. In other words, souls choose their parents to learn from them as well as to teach them.

Parents, extended family members, and close friends are generally part of the same soul group from one lifetime to another although they may manifest in different roles in one another's lives. Given this notion, it is quite possible, likely even, that your kids actually did choose you rather than the converse. And they chose you specifically based on what they needed to learn from you, and what you need to learn from them to help you both evolve as spiritual beings.

Karma, the vehicle through which life lessons are taught, is present from one lifetime into the next and may be responsible for some of the experiences that humans are destined to face. We cannot save our children from their karma any more than our parents could save us from our own. Some of us enter our new lifecycle with positive karma fueling our new life, and others are still working to pay off old karmic debts from a past carnation or two. In short, we are only partially responsible for our children's wellbeing. A force much stronger than any of us as individuals is at play here too.

All children are born with a personality of their own accompanied by free will. They come into this world with a will to survive, to fight back, and to triumph over others. It is basically our job to civilize and socialize them, and to further their ability to love themselves and others. It is our job to teach them to be good people. Often we go about teaching them to be good people without feeling like we are fully good people ourselves, because indeed we may not be yet, and this alone is enough to fill us with incredible doubt and fear about their future, and sometimes our own as well. As Lao-Tzu so eloquently stated, "Being deeply loved by someone gives you strength; loving someone deeply gives you courage." Such it is with parents and kids, loving one another gives us the courage to do things that neither of us ever thought we could do.

Raising Loving Kids

Again, I am no expert on childrearing, but I have born witness to several examples of excellent and loving parenting in my life. These parents were able to raise loving, giving children who have grown up to make a worthy contribution to the world around them. As I think about the way in which these children were raised I have noticed a number of commonalities in their parents' methods. Although the families I am thinking about come from different races, communities, ethnic origins, spiritual beliefs and compositions (single parent, male-female parents, same sex parents, foster parents, and grandparents or relatives as parents), they have all managed to raise stellar humans in about the same way. Here is a brief summary of how they have done it.

1. Teach your children respect for themselves and others. This includes manners, acceptance of differences, the ability to see others as individuals who have the right to their own thinking and beliefs, and a high regard for human life, including their own.
2. Teach your children to love, not just by loving them and modeling a loving attitude towards your fellow man but also by involving them in caring for others who are less fortunate or more vulnerable than themselves. Point out how by helping others you earn high self-esteem.
3. Teach them to avoid selfishness in any form. Life is about giving of yourself to others whether it is in the form of sharing one's toys or giving time, a helping hand, or a listening ear to another person.
4. Listen deeply when your children talk and be inquisitive about their thoughts. Be fully present when you spend time with them and show them how important they are to you by tuning out all of the distractions that rob them of your full attention.
5. Let them learn from their mistakes. Do not rescue them from their own bad acts. Behaviors have consequences. The primary way in which children learn not to do hurtful things to themselves and others is to suffer some pain or loss due to their actions. Let your children explain their own actions and pay their own consequences when they screw up.
6. Hold your children accountable for doing what they promise to do. Children learn to be reliable when they are counted on to follow through and keep their word. Model accountability by admitting to and taking responsibility for your own mistakes and following through on your own promises to the extent possible.
7. Do not lie to your children or in their presence. If they ask you about something that shouldn't concern them explain that it is not something you are willing to discuss, but don't lie. Children learn to be trustworthy by watching and listening to their parents.
8. Let your children know that you will always love them and be there for them no matter what they might do, but expect the best from them in every situation. Guide them as to what their best choices might be. If they listen they will benefit, if not, they will suffer the consequences if they turn out to be wrong. From this process they will learn to make good decisions.
9. Cultivate a sense of humor in your children. Make sure they know how to laugh at the little slights life offers up. Encourage them to laugh at themselves when they make small blunders. Teach them to count their blessings when they are down. Knowing how to regard the world with a positive perspective is a great gift to pass along to your little ones.
10. Teach your children to manage stress and conflict. Unfortunately the world is full of bullies and bad guys. If your child is constantly defeated by those stronger and meaner than they themselves it won't be long before they lose faith in their own ability to protect themselves. Children need to learn to prevail over temptation and threat to believe themselves to be strong and worthy, so teach them to fight, but to always fight fair.

The Nature of Conflict

In order to teach your children to deal with conflict constructively, it is necessary for you to know how conflict develops. Conflict is a process, not an event. Conflict becomes apparent with the advent of a trigger event. This event may be large and significant or small and unassuming. Regardless of its size, this event causes a conflict to surface and become apparent to others. The trigger event is sometimes referred to as "the straw that broke the camel's back." After the conflict surfaces, it begins to develop.

At the peak of a conflict any issues that are resolved to the satisfaction of all parties will simply dissipate. Any issues that remain unresolved will require those who are still concerned and upset to adapt to the current situation. The concern doesn't disappear just because it is no longer discussed. It merely goes into an undercurrent where the dissatisfaction tends to grow and may even take on a life of its own. If you find that someone in your household is angry all of the time, it might have something to do with the way they deal with conflict. Unresolved conflict never really goes away, but it can simmer beneath the surface for lengthy periods before surfacing again. Unresolved anger can nearly always be linked to unresolved conflict that is going unaddressed.

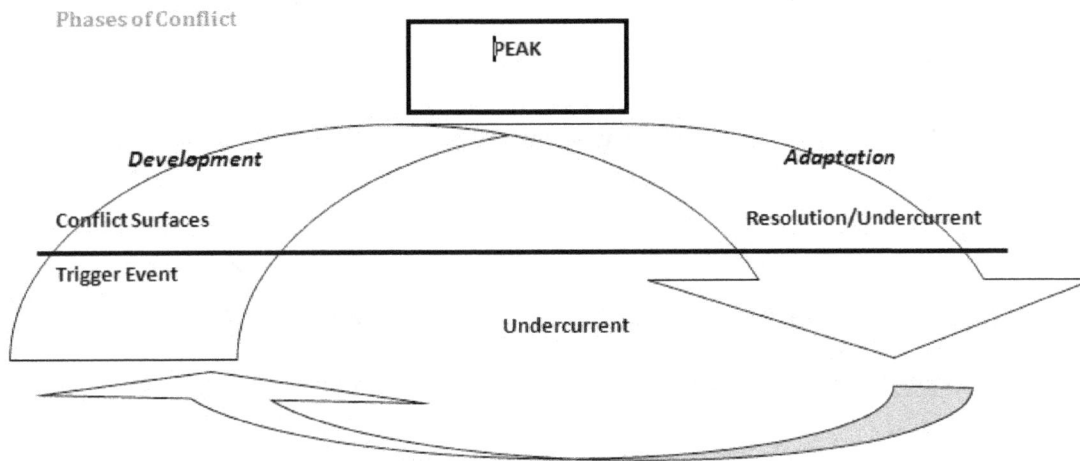

Phases of Conflict

PEAK

Development

Adaptation

Conflict Surfaces

Resolution/Undercurrent

Trigger Event

Undercurrent

Fighting Fair

Conflict management is the basis for fair fighting. Normally, when we find ourselves in a conflict situation we respond in a personality dependent sort of way. Some with yell, threaten, and pound their fist. Others will withdraw and go conduct research in an effort to prove the other guy wrong. Still others will just stuff the conflict down and pretend nothing is wrong, or attempt to laugh it away by making a joke about it. Although all of these reactions to conflict work in some situations, they are not universal and applicable to every situation.

There are truly only five ways to manage conflict, and rather than to react in a personal manner to it, we need to respond to it in a thoughtful and intelligent manner. The following model suggests that we need to respond to conflict by weighing the importance of the issue at hand against the importance of the relationship with the other person. If the issue is more important than maintaining a warm relationship you need to assert yourself, but if the relationship is more important than the issue at hand, you need to cooperate.

When neither the issue nor its importance to your relationship with another person is obvious, it is probably best to say nothing and **avoid** the conflict. If the relationship is more important than the issue you are safe in **accommodating** the other person and giving in to what they want. Use **compromise** when the issue and relationship are of equal importance but there is room to be flexible and engage in some give and take with the other person. **Collaboration** can occur when both parties to the conflict can agree to a mutually acceptable outcome and seek to resolve the issue while maintaining the relationship because both are important. It involves brainstorming together to find alternatives that will lead to the agreed upon result. It is only necessary to **compete** with another person when the issue at hand is more important than maintaining a relationship with the other person. Only compete when you are prepared to sacrifice your relationship with the other person.

Five Ways to Manage Conflict

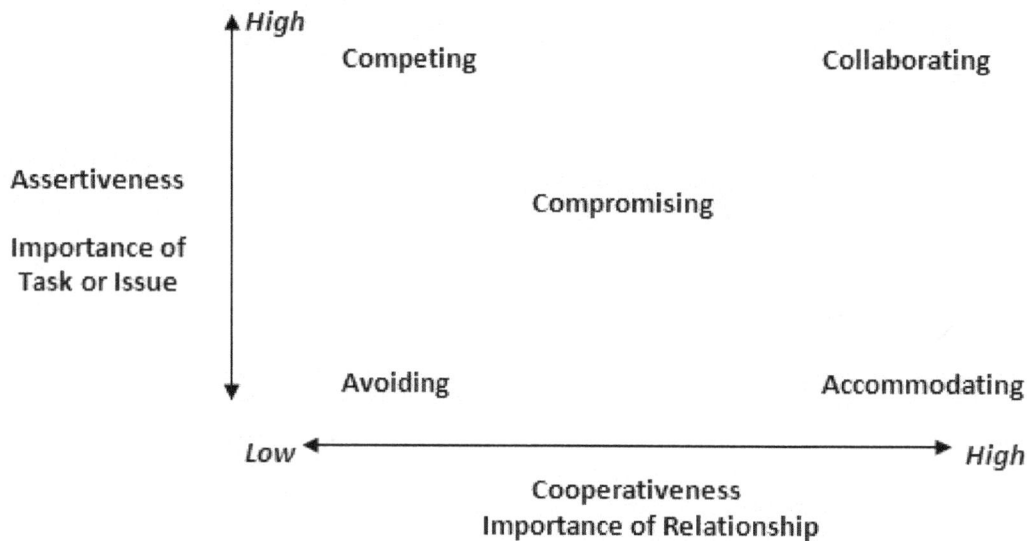

1. **Avoid**—Neither you nor I satisfy our concerns.
2. **Accommodate**—I satisfy your concerns at my expense.
3. **Compete**—I satisfy my concerns at your expense.
4. **Compromise**—We give up some of our concerns for other concerns.
5. **Collaborate**—Together we discover alternatives to satisfy all concerns.

Courage

Managing conflict requires courage. Simply deciding which conflict management strategy will work best to resolve the conflict at hand is not enough. Think about a time when you knew exactly what you should do in the middle of a conflict, but your fear stopped you from following through. Sometimes we fear losing face, or appearing weak, or backing down, so we keep competing when we should be accommodating. Other times we give up too quickly fearing that we are being pushy or obnoxious or annoying when we need to stand our ground on an important issue. In the words of Lady Diana Spencer, "Courage is not the absence of fear but rather the judgment that something is more important than fear. The brave may not live forever but the cautious do not live at all."

Vow to resolve your issues, whether they be related to your relationship with your kids, your workmates, your partner or your neighbor. Weigh your options, select the strategy that will best address the issue at hand, plan out your approach, and then confront the conflict head on. Know that you are teaching your children how to stand up for their beliefs while treating others with respect during conflict as you demonstrate the courage to appropriately deal with the grievances in your own life.

Parent courageously. Be brave enough to allow your children to make their own mistakes, and to own them. Have the courage to stand up to your children when you believe they are wrong, and support them when you think they are right, regardless of the opinions or opposition of others. No one wants to live in constant conflict with their kids, although lots of families do just that. Pick your battles carefully, but address the important issues with an unstoppable will to succeed. Even if you don't earn your children's gratitude you will earn their respect.

Courageous Confrontation

If you are a mother please focus on a conflict involving one of your children. If you are not a parent please focus on any conflict that is troubling you. By answering these questions about the conflict you will be able formulate a plan to tackle the conflict in a targeted and respectful way.

Confronting Conflict
Describe a current conflict that you would like to bring to resolution. Say who is involved and what you believe is the problem or issue.
Now look at the conflict from the other party's view. Who would they say was involved and how would they describe the problem or issue?
Is your relationship important to both of you? Why or why not?
Is the issue or problem at hand important to both of you? Why or why not?
Do you both want to see about the same outcome once the problem is resolved?
Would you both be willing to compromise if you want different outcomes?
Based on your answers, which conflict management strategy will you select to address the issue?
How will you help the other party feel supported and understood during the confrontation?
What will you ask for in order for you to be satisfied with the resolution of the conflict and leave feeling respected?
How will you display courage during and after the confrontation?
If this attempt to resolve the conflict is unsuccessful what will you do on an ongoing basis to best manage the conflict until it can be resolved?

Not all conflict is resolvable, especially not on the first try. Often people, whether young or old, will stubbornly cling to their position, or fail to behave respectfully with the full knowledge that they are wrong. Fear prevents them from moving forward. Don't give up on teaching your children the valuable lessons you need to pass along. Resistance is futile in the face of a persistent mother!

A Real Woman

Kelly's 13-year-old daughter Cam is bright and beautiful. She does well in school, and is funny, active, exuberant and athletic. Kelly considers herself fortunate that Cam is not yet interested in make-up, piercings, tattoos and boys like some of her friends, and she fiercely loves her daughter. But with puberty approaching Cam is getting to be difficult to live with. Lately Cam has started to exhibit a quick temper and angers at the mere suggestion that it is time to do her chores. Given Cam's propensity for disorganization, the house is strewn from front to rear with Cam's possessions and her room looks like a hurricane hit it. Dirty and clean clothes lay together in a huge pile beside her bed. Each morning Cam can be heard screaming because she can't find anything to wear that isn't rumbled or mismatched. When Kelly suggests that she clean her room and hang up her clothes Cam screams even louder.

Today started with the usual search for a clean outfit even though Kelly had recently done laundry. Add to that Kelly tripped over Cam's book bag lying in the center of a dark hallway causing her to smash into the wall and bruise her elbow, so the morning drama took a particularly ugly turn. "Damn Cam," Kelly shouted as she slung the misplaced book bag onto Cam's bed, "Are you trying to kill me?"
"Are you trying to kill me?" Cam screamed in reply. "I didn't throw my book bag at you! I can't help it that you are blind and clumsy and don't watch where you are going!" With that Kelly saw red. "You are sloppy, ungrateful

and disrespectful," Kelly accused. "I work hard to buy you nice things and you just throw them around like they mean nothing to you. You are so lazy that you won't even hang up your clothes and you refuse to do your daily chores and help me keep the house picked up."

"It's not MY house, it's YOUR house, so you should keep it clean! I am not your maid," Cam declared. "You are grounded until your room is cleaned, your closet is organized, and all of your stuff is picked up throughout OUR house and put where it belongs!" Kelly announced as she scurried to get away before Cam could respond.

Throughout the day Kelly felt upset due to the feud with Cam, and by the time she got home from work she was ready to discuss the situation in a calm and reasonable manner. "Come and have some cookies and milk with me before you start your chores," Kelly suggested to Cam. With a show of skepticism Cam accepted the invitation. "So you would rather eat cookies with me than have me do my chores?" Cam inquired.

"Yes I would," replied Kelly. "I can understand why you don't like to do chores. I don't like doing them either, but the longer things pile up, the more difficult it is to find the things I need and to clean up the mess so I make myself do it daily so I can keep up with it." "I know what you mean," Cam replied. "I don't even know where to start on my room."

"Could you use some help from the Queen of Clean?" Kelly smiled. "I am willing to come and get you started if you promise to pick up your stuff daily without reminder and keep your clothes organized after we get them put away." "I promise," Cam agreed. "I really hate it when I can't find what I want to wear in the morning." "Bring the cookies," Kelly instructed as she headed towards Cam's room. "We will need a sugar buzz to make a dent in this mess."

Although Kelly and Cam still have their differences the morning drama is no longer a part of their daily ritual. Now Kelly sticks her head in Cam's doorway daily and compliments her neat room and her cool outfit, and Cam leaves for school without the scowl that used to occupy her face each day. Everyone loves a day that starts that way!

The Confidence Game

"Staying silent is like a slow growing cancer to the soul and a trait of a true coward. There is nothing intelligent about not standing up for yourself. You may not win every battle. However, everyone will at least know what you stood for—YOU." Shannon L. Alder

Women currently hold 24 (4.8%) of CEO positions at Standards & Poor's 500 companies. In the US Congress you will find 104 (19.4%) of the seats occupied by women. Women own 28.8% of the businesses. The median income of full-time workers was $42,800 for men, compared to $34,700 for women. The U.S. population is 50.8% female.

Do these statistics sound like mind numbing numbers to you? If so, that is exactly how the male run establishment in the United States would like you to react. They don't want you to look too closely at the numbers, or to think too much about them. And if you do study the numbers it is hoped that you will feel overwhelmed by them. After all, what can you, and other women like you really do to overcome the wage disparity between men and women? What can you do to put more women in Congress or aid in the rise of women to top positions in big firms?

Why do these numbers exist? If women compose over half the population in this country then why don't they command at least 50% of the wealth? Why aren't half of the businesses owned by women? Why don't women elect other women to Congress? Will women ever progress to equal status to men if men continue to run the show? I think not.

How did men manage this? Are males superior to females? Are they smarter? Faster? Stronger? More intimidating? More ruthless? More clever? What is it? I think it is that men feel more entitled than woman. They feel truly deserving of power, respect and money. They will stop at nothing to assure their rightful place on the planet, in dominion over all living things.

Given this mindset how can women possibly compete? How can they become great when the odds are stacked against them? Here are some ways that we are trying.

- More women are getting a college education. In the 1970's men comprised 71% of all college students, but today they are in the minority of college attendees at 46.2%.
- More men drop out of college annually than do women, making 58% of all college graduates female.
- On average girls graduate from high school with a GPA of 3.10 while boys graduate with a 2.90. Besting boys in earning grades is something that females excel at from kindergarten to graduate school, but a woman who gets a 4.0 GPA in high school will only be worth about as much, income-wise, as a man who got a 2.0.
- Women are viewed as being significantly better than men at working out compromises, being ethical and honest, working to improve the quality of life for others, and standing up for their beliefs. Men are more willing to take risks than women, and excel at negotiating profitable deals.

Interestingly, women tend to excel in 15 out of 16 leadership competencies when they finally do win a leadership role within an organization or open their own business. Men are better strategists than women, but women take the prize for developing the potential of others, and getting the best business results.

The Top 16 Competencies Top Leaders Exemplify Most

	Male Mean Percentile	Female Mean Percentile	T value
Takes Initiative	48	56	-11.58
Practices Self-Development	48	55	-9.45
Displays High Integrity and Honesty	48	55	-9.28
Drives for Results	48	54	-8.84
Develops Others	48	54	-7.94
Inspires and Motivates Others	49	54	-7.53
Builds Relationships	49	54	-7.15
Collaboration and Teamwork	49	53	-6.14
Establishes Stretch Goals	49	53	-5.41
Champions Change	49	53	-4.48
Solves Problems and Analyzes Issues	50	52	-2.53
Communicates Powerfully and Prolifically	50	52	-2.47
Connects the Group to the Outside World	50	51	-0.78
Innovates	50	51	-0.76
Technical or Professional Expertise	50	51	-0.11
Develops Strategic Perspective	51	49	2.79

Source: Zenger Folkman Inc., 2011

In short ladies, no guts, no glory. Men beat out women in only three categories. They are more proficient at taking risks than women, are better at developing strategy, and studies show that they work more hours than women due to having less responsibility for home and family than their female counterparts. One would think that excelling in practically all business skill sets would level the playing field for men and women, but it is clearly not so.

Let's break it down. What causes men to be better at strategizing and risk taking than women? In short, it is confidence. When a person feels entitled to something they tend to go after it with a vengeance. Men feel entitled to success, they feel they deserve it, and are willing to gamble everything to get it. Women, on the other hand, tend to believe that they must earn their place in the world, not simply demand it.

Should women even try to compete with men to become higher wage earners, known leaders, and money moguls? Perhaps not, unless you are not content with your current station in life. There is no more noble pursuit than to be a good mom, daughter, friend and community member, even if it is done without fair compensation. But what if you feel you are worth more, could do more, or deserve more for your effort than you are currently receiving? Then it is time to up your game and behave in ways that show you are a force to be reckoned with. It is time to advocate for you, both at work and at home.

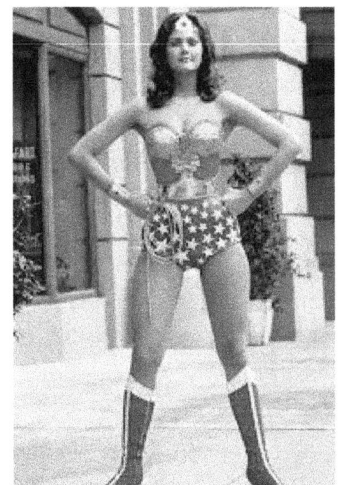

The Superhero Pose

During an episode of Grey's Anatomy, Dr. Amelia Sheppard was found by a colleague standing in the scrub room before an important and nearly impossible surgery. Hands on hips, feet in a wide stance, chest puffed out, shoulders back, and chin held high, Dr. Sheppard was assuming her "Superhero pose." Unashamed, she continued to hold the stance and explained to the onlooker that recent research coming out of Harvard University, The University of Oregon, and The University of Texas shows that assuming the superhero pose for just two minutes will positively charge your neuro-endrocrine levels. Scientists tested the saliva of the power posers and affirmed that just 120 seconds of powerful posture increases testosterone (dominance hormone) about 20%, while dropping Cortisol (stress hormone) about 25% in both men and women.

Although there are a number of power poses that one can assume before a difficult task, or as a daily morning habit, the pose shown here seems to give you the most bang for your buck. Practice it daily and eventually the pose will work its way into your daily posture. Look more powerful and you will feel more confident. Feel more confident and you will improve your performance in the male dominated areas of risk taking and strategic thinking.

Negotiation Skills

Although feeling more confident is highly beneficial and feels spectacular, if you truly want to become more powerful at work and at home you may also need to build your skills in the areas of risk taking and strategic perceptual development. Learning to negotiate effectively will enhance both skills sets, and will also help you prevail when it is time to ask for a raise at work, or buy a car for the rock bottom price. Learning to negotiate is tantamount to learning to handle conflict effectively so negotiation skills can also do double duty as conflict mediation techniques.

Most women have been negotiating all of their lives. As children, we negotiated for attention, allowances, and special treats. As teenagers, we negotiated for driving privileges, curfews, and going to parties. As adults, we negotiate for jobs, raises, and to get some help with household chores, just to name a few. The negotiation process remains the same, no matter what our age or what we're negotiating for. Understanding that process is what will help make you a more successful negotiator.

Your personal negotiation style is a critical variable in bargaining. If you don't know what your instincts and intuition will tell you to do under different conditions, you will have trouble planning effective strategies and responses. Psychologists have isolated five basic negotiation styles based on how people handle interpersonal conflict.

- **Competitors** – Competitors like to win and often believe that the end justifies the means. They're usually willing to take big risks on the chance that it will pay off for them.
- **Collaborators** – Collaborators try to solve problems and find a solution that ensures everyone gets all of his/her needs met.
- **Compromisers** – Compromisers are interested in maintaining productive relationships with others. They favor agreements that give all parties an equitable part of each and every item on the table.
- **Accommodators** – Accommodators are likely to want to solve everyone's problems. They trust the other party to be fair and equitable, but since that doesn't always happen, sometimes the accommodator comes away empty handed.
- **Avoiders** – Avoiders strongly dislike conflict of any kind. They have distaste for games or situations that have winners or losers and they try to dodge situations that have the prospect of open disagreement.

Which type of negotiator are you? Is your negotiation style serving you well? Remember Shannon, the "people pleaser" from the Stress Mess chapter? She is an Accommodator. Shannon just wants everyone to happy and to get what they want...everyone except herself, who often walks away empty handed after giving her all to others. Avoiders, first cousins to Accommodators, are others who generally fail to get their own needs met because they are unwilling to step up and state their own needs. Men who have an entitlement mentality generally assume the Competitor role, and they often get their own needs met, but at a high price, because others are left unsatisfied and may even want to seek revenge on the person they believe has taken what is rightfully theirs. Compromisers end up with about half of what they want and need, and seldom feel like winners at the end of the day.

If you said you are a Collaborator, you are someone who goes into a conflict or a negotiation with confidence that there is a workable solution that can be achieved in every situation. You consult genuinely and widely with others to surface their unique perspectives on the problem at hand, and you respect their input as well as your own. Collaborators are usually successful at finding lasting remedies to daily issues regardless of how much time must be invested in getting a result that is win-win for all involved. The drawback to collaboration is that it might be more time consuming than the other strategic stances, but isn't it worth a bit more time and effort to get it right and assure satisfaction for all?

Brian Tracy gives us 14 characteristics that need to be present in the attitude and behavior of a successful negotiator.

1. A person who continuously looks for creative ways to better the price, the terms, or the situation.
2. A person who views the process of negotiation as a life-long process.
3. A person who uses bargaining, trading, and compromising in all interactions with other people.
4. A person who views the process of negotiation as an ongoing, never-ending process of interaction with other people.
5. A person who is open-minded, adaptive and creative.
6. A person who is willing to consider all types of options and possibilities.
7. A person who avoids taking fixed positions.
8. A person who is fluid, flexible and quick to identify mutual goals.
9. A person who looks for areas of compromise early on in order to get off to a smooth start.
10. A person who is cooperative, rather than competitive.
11. A person who continuously seeks collaborative solutions.
12. A person who looks for benefits for all parties.
13. A person who looks for newer, easier, innovative and unusual solutions for all parties to get what they want.
14. A person who is honest, direct and non-manipulative.

Let's try it. Think of something in your life that isn't currently a good deal for you. Are you doing the lion's share of the housework in your family? Are you underpaid at work? Is there a friend or relative that treats you as though you are a servant but seldom helps you when you need a hand? Find an issue that you would like to negotiate in an attempt to get a better deal. Begin by stating your issue clearly and in measureable terms. For example, you might say, "I would like a 10% raise in salary within the next 12 months," or "I would like my spouse to do all of the spring yard work this year while I do the spring house cleaning." To plan your negotiation, answer the questions posed which will take you through a standard negotiating process.

Issue to be negotiated

Step One: Understand the Other Party
What are your common interests or goals in the situation?
How can your position be a good option for him/her?
What are the possible objections s/he might raise?
How will you counter those objections?
Step Two: Know your Bottom Line

Why are you negotiating?
What are your goals and objectives?
What specific conditions do you want to exist when an agreement is reached?
How much less are you willing to accept?
Step Three: Leverage
What do you have that they want?
How badly do they want it?
Can they get it anywhere else?
Step Four: Information Exchange
How will you establish rapport at the onset of the negotiation?
What will you ask to learn the interests and perceptions of the other party regarding the issue?
How will you present your leverage to the other party?
Step Four: Proposing and Countering
What will you say to get the other party to make the first offer?
What will you say to counter with a request for a better offer if needed?
What concessions are you willing to make to preserve a good relationship with the other party?
Step Five: Agreement
How will you seal the deal? In writing? Verbally? A handshake?
How long will the agreement be in force before being renegotiated?
What will be the penalty for violating the agreement in the future?

Congratulations! You have written a complete negotiation plan to get something you want or need in your life presently. Now set an appointment to speak with the other party and let the negotiation begin! As you look at your negotiation plan do you see evidence of strategic thinking? You are building your skills in this male dominated area while you are seeking a better deal for yourself. Now that is what I call multi-tasking at its best!

Speaking of multi-tasking, women are naturally better at it than men. As mentioned earlier, our brains can accommodate it better than a man's brain. That does not, however, mean we have to engage in this practice 24/7/365. Multi-tasking is difficult for both men and women. It splits your attention and makes it more likely that you will make errors or forget vital aspects of a task. It requires that you interrupt yourself numerous times over a short period, and it extends the time it takes to complete each task.

Since women are clearly superior in this area, men may assume that multi-tasking is easy for you, and therefore expect you to do it on a consistent basis. If this is the case for you, it might be advantageous to set some firm, kind limits on those who expect you to be a multi-tasking marvel. This is where confidence comes into play again. In both negotiating and limit setting you must not only feel confident, but you must also sound and appear confident if you are to prevail. Using assertive talking skills will help you convey your confidence to others in a manner that is integrity-filled and effective.

Assertive Talking Skills

Being assertive is more than a talking technique. It is a mindset, one that says you deserve to be treated as an equal, and respected as a competent individual. An assertive stance is one that says, "I'm okay, and you are okay too." In contrast, aggression suggests that "I'm okay and you are not," and passivity supposes that "You're okay, but I am not." In order to convey a congruent and consistent assertive message one must feel like an assertive person. Here is your "Bill of Rights" when it comes to asserting yourself. It is the thinking that allows you to become a more assertive person.

Assertiveness Bill of Rights

- You have a right to put yourself first sometimes.
- You have a right to have your own opinion and convictions.
- You have a right to change your mind.
- You have a right to be treated fairly and to protest if you're not.
- You have a right to receive recognition and praise for your work and accomplishments.
- You have a right not to take responsibility for someone else's problem.
- You have the right to be the ultimate judge of yourself and your behavior.
- You have the right to offer no excuses or reasons to justify your behavior.
- You have the right to make mistakes and be responsible for them and learn from them.
- You have the right to set your own priorities.
- You have the right to refuse a request without feeling guilty.
- You have the right to ask for what you want (knowing that others have the right to refuse).
- You have a right to say no without giving reasons why or apologizing.
- You have the right to not assert your rights.

Adapted with permission from Manuel J. Smith. *When I say no I feel guilty*. New York: Dial Press, 1975.

How do you feel about your assertiveness rights? Are there any that you don't currently exercise? Do you disagree that you are entitled to all of these rights? If so, you also have the right not to assert your rights! But really, you have the right to be human, and regardless of how hard you try to be more than that, you cannot, so you may as well give up the guilt trips that you send yourself on now, and simply accept that you have the right to be imperfect without apology. The minute you integrate that fact in your thinking you will notice that you immediately feel calmer and more at peace. It is a real confidence booster to understand that your best is good enough, and that no one has the right to expect more than that from you.

"We need women who are so strong they can be gentle, so educated they can be humble, so fierce they can be compassionate, so passionate they can be rational, and so disciplined they can be free."

— Kavita Ramdas

Assertive behavior involves respecting other people's rights while not allowing others to infringe yours. Although there are a variety of advanced assertive talking skills, the one most women need to learn first is how to say "no" with comfort and self-assurance. Here are some tips on how to set limits on unreasonable requests from others. Saying no does not imply that you reject another person; you are simply refusing a request.

- When saying no, it is important to be direct, concise, and to the point.
- Begin your answer with the word "No" so it is not ambiguous.
- Make your answer short and to the point.
- Don't give a long explanation.
- Be honest, direct and firm.
- Don't say, "I'm sorry, but..."

Accompany the word "no" with assertive body language and you will discover that few will want to argue with you or attempt to manipulate you into changing your mind. And if they are silly enough to try stay strong and don't succumb to their guilt inducing efforts.

Assertive body language includes:

- Maintaining direct eye contact.
- Maintaining an erect posture.
- Speaking clearly and audibly.
- Not using a soft, whiny, or muffled voice.
- Using facial expressions and gestures to add emphasis to your words.

In essence, what an assertive response does it to protect your boundaries while simultaneously assuring that you are not disrespecting someone else's boundaries. Boundaries define your personal space, your possessions, your ideas and feelings, and your needs. They protect you from unwarranted intrusion.

The key to speaking assertively is to begin your sentences with the word "I." The word "you" can be interpreted as blaming or fault-finding, while the word "I" allows you to take ownership of yourself, your thoughts and your actions. "I want…, I will…, I won't…, I can't…I need…, I am willing," are all good sentence starters when responding to others who are trying to bend your will to their own. Being assertive is not difficult, and will become increasingly easier for you with a little practice.

Assert Yourself

By being assertive you can neutralize criticism without apology, and end manipulative behavior directed at you by refusing to buy into it. Most of us have at least one major critic in our lives whether that person is at work or at home, and it is probably time to interrupt their pattern by refusing to be affected by their negative input into your life.

The very next time someone is critical of you use one of the techniques listed here to fend off the criticism without allowing it to damage your self-confidence.

- Agree with the truth - Find a statement in the criticism that is truthful and agree with that statement. Don't apologize, simply agree and move on.
- Agree in principle - Agree with the general truth in a logical statement such as, "That makes sense."
- Workable Compromise - When your self-respect is not in question offer a workable compromise.

Immediately after issuing an assertive response pay attention to how you feel. You will find that you feel empowered, not guilty, sad or sorry. Accepting your flaws, mistakes and shortcomings without protest or excuse is a very liberating action, so practice it without embarrassment or hesitation, and you will find yourself growing in confidence day by day.

A Real Woman

Everyone liked Maria. After all, what was not to like? She was quick to agree with everyone, and if she couldn't bring herself to be agreeable she simply remained silent. She was good at making herself invisible in tense situations, and seldom drew fire like her more expressive coworkers. Her meekness worked out well for most everyone but Maria. Don't think she didn't notice that she always ended up with the dirtiest jobs, the smallest piece of cake on her birthday, and the most marginal raises compared to others in her work group. Passivity was the key to peace she told herself, although that was becoming harder to believe with each passing day.

Then came the red letter day that she would never forget. Stan, a particularly obnoxious coworker approached her desk with a grin. "Hey Babe," he called out, "Could you do me a big favor and fix the errors on my monthly report for me? I never get it right and you will be able to make the corrections they want much faster than me!"

"Make your own damned corrections," Maria snapped. "I have work of my own to do!" Undeterred by the shocked look on his face, Maria continued. "If you weren't so oblivious to the policy you wouldn't have a ton of errors to correct each month. Do it right the first time Moron, and then you won't have to worry about how much time it takes to do it over!"

Stan beat a hasty retreat from her cubicle and Maria was immediately overcome with guilt. Moments later her intercom buzzed. Her supervisor needed to see her...now! She was sure she was about to be fired, but at that moment she wasn't sure that she even cared.

Maria's supervisor didn't fire her, but he did patronize her. He suggested she take a vacation day and do something nice for herself to alleviate her crankiness. Seething, Maria thanked the supervisor and scurried from the building. At home, Maria was at a loss as to what to do next. After an hour of pacing and muttering to herself she flopped down on the sofa and turned on the TV. India Arie was on a daytime talk show singing one of her lesser known songs, "Come Back to the Middle."

Exactly! That is precisely what she needed to do, Maria realized. Passivity was giving her ulcers, and aggression was jeopardizing her livelihood. There must be a middle ground position that would get her a better result. She got to work immediately. First she wrote down all the things in her life that dissatisfied her. Next to each item she wrote an assertive sentence to be used to request a better deal. She finished her list by choosing the top three items that she intended to address first, and started making phone calls.

She scheduled a meeting with her supervisor to discuss a raise, called her sister to let her know that she would no longer babysit free for her every weekend, but offered to host a birthday party for her niece the following weekend, something that she really wanted to do. To finish off her day of liberation she phoned the veterinarian and canceled the $200 teeth cleaning that he had insisted she schedule for her dog, and took the money she had saved to cover the procedure and purchased a new outfit for herself.

Maria is a happy person now. When others attempt to impose on her she asks herself whether she really wants or needs to fulfill their request. If the answer is yes, she grants the favor. If not, she politely refuses the request without guilt or apology. She no longer feels resentful towards others for taking advantage of her, because she doesn't allow them to do so anymore.

That Healing Feeling

"The wound is the place where the Light enters you." Rumi

Almost daily I encounter woman who are wounded. Their wounds are the results of family and sexual violence, child abuse, racism, sexism, ageism, crime and war. The wounds are deep, and for some they may never heal. Many suffer from Post-traumatic Stress Disorder (PTSD), a condition that, if severe enough, permanently alters your personality. Some of the wounds are fresh, and some ancient, but saddest of all, some are ongoing. How can you recover from something that is still happening to you?

Although I am a survivor of domestic violence myself, I am astonished when I facilitate the topic *Addressing Domestic Violence* and find that over 45% of the women in the room have been injured by family violence. The injuries occur to mind, body and soul. Most are the target of the violence perpetrated against them, but a few are injured by proxy. One grandmother cried throughout the training session knowing that her son is perpetrating violence against his wife in the presence of the children. Another woman revealed that her husband killed his mistress while they were married. And yet another spoke for the first time in nearly two decades about the day when her boyfriend killed her three-year-old son.

Violence of any type has an indescribable reach. It transcends generations and family ties and affects even the friends and acquaintances of those who experience it. Returning soldiers still scan the roads near their homes looking for explosive devices that they know in their rational minds they left behind in the Middle East. They return home different people than they were when they left, and those who are closest to them mourn the loss of the person they used to be. The pain is real and pervasive for all who are connected to them.

We spend lots of time talking about violence in the United States. It dominates the evening news and is the subject of gossip when it occurs, but we say little about how to heal from it. So let's talk about it. Has your life, or the life of someone you love been affected by violence? Did you know that PTSD is common after even short exposure to violent acts? Did you know that it is possible to heal even if you have been diagnosed with post-traumatic stress disorder?

PTSD

The National Center for PTSD reports that 60% of all adults will suffer from at least one significant trauma in their lifetime. During a traumatic event, you think that your life or others' lives are in danger. You may feel afraid or feel that you have no control over what is happening around you. Most people have some stress-related reactions after a traumatic event; but, not everyone gets PTSD. If your reactions don't go away over time and they disrupt your life, you may have PTSD. Whether or not you get PTSD depends on many things:

- How intense the trauma was or how long it lasted
- If you were injured or lost someone important to you
- How close you were to the event and how strong your reaction was
- How much you felt in control of events
- How much help and support you got after the event

There are four types of symptoms of PTSD:

- Reliving the event (also called re-experiencing symptoms)—You may have bad memories or nightmares. You even may feel like you're going through the event again. This is called a flashback.

- Avoiding situations that remind you of the event—You may try to avoid situations or people that trigger memories of the traumatic event. You may even avoid talking or thinking about the event.
- Negative changes in beliefs and feelings—The way you think about yourself and others may change because of the trauma. You may feel fear, guilt, or shame. Or, you may not be interested in activities you used to enjoy. This is another way to avoid memories.
- Feeling keyed up—You may be jittery, or always alert and on the lookout for danger. Or, you may have trouble concentrating or sleeping.

Do you have PTSD or know someone who does? Although Rumi (quoted below the title of this chapter) believes that a wound is the place that the light enters you, it may be just the opposite for a wound that results in PTSD. In this case, the wound injures your soul, or at least your ability to communicate with your soul. Peace of mind, which comes from communicating with your soul seems impossible to achieve, and instead you remain in the tortured memories held by your own consciousness. It is for that reason that I would recommend that you see a mental health professional if you think you have PTSD. A therapist can help you control and organize your thoughts and can assist you in desensitizing yourself to the fear and pain of trauma so you can move past it and let the light come in.

There are different types of psychotherapy:

- Cognitive behavioral therapy (CBT) is the most effective treatment for PTSD. There are different types of CBT, such as cognitive therapy and exposure therapy.
- One type is Cognitive Processing Therapy (CPT) where you learn skills to understand how trauma changed your thoughts and feelings.
- Another type is Prolonged Exposure (PE) therapy where you talk about your trauma repeatedly until memories are no longer upsetting. You also go to places that are safe, but that you have been staying away from because they are related to the trauma.
- A similar kind of therapy is called Eye Movement Desensitization and Reprocessing (EMDR), which involves focusing on sounds or hand movements while you talk about the trauma.

You know more about the nature of your trauma, and the depth of your pain than anyone else, so research the type of therapy that you feel will best aid in your healing. Interview several therapists, discuss the therapeutic approach they utilize, and select the person you feel most as ease with. If s/he is to help you it is essential that you feel you can trust the therapist to guide you safely through the healing process. The journey back to health can occur slowly or quickly, but you will know when you are there. You will be at peace, and you will be able to access the voice of your soul without it being distorted by the static vibrations of fear and pain.

Forgiveness

There is another therapy you can try that doesn't require professional guidance. You can practice forgiveness. Begin with yourself. Almost all trauma victims blame themselves at some level. In an attempt to gain control of a situation that is traumatizing and overwhelming, women often begin to mentally criticize and blame themselves. Whatever you believe your role and responsibility was in the situation that led to your victimization, forgive yourself for it. I know this is a propensity of women because I hear it consistently. Women in domestic violence class blame the victim, even if they later reveal that they have been victims themselves.

You cannot hope to forget a painful memory until you forgive yourself for your responsibility in the matter, even if you are imagining that you are responsible for an aspect of the situation that you had no control over. The grandmother who is mortified by the fact that her son is abusing his wife is imagining that she could have said or done something differently while raising the boy that would have prevented his adult actions. The woman whose toddler was killed by her boyfriend imagines that she could have saved the child had she returned home instead of going to work on that fated day.

It makes no difference whether a woman's responsibility in her victimization is real or imagined, she must come to closure with it before she will be able to move on. It is also helpful if those around her forgive her for her perceived shortcomings. When football star Ray Rice knocked his fiancé unconscious in an elevator men and women across the country speculated out loud about what she did that caused him to punch her. This sort of victim-blaming crosses gender, socio-economic and cultural lines. Even the mother of a victim of violence might blame her for being senseless, baiting the perpetrator, being in the wrong place, wearing the wrong thing, or trusting the wrong person.

If those around you refuse to forgive you for "getting yourself into this mess," you need to forgive yourself. Understand that those who love you are trying to help you avoid the same situation in the future. Forgive them for their misunderstanding of the reality of your situation. Your friends and relatives will have a difficult time, however, forgiving your role and responsibility if you are living in a violent situation that you refuse to leave. In order to be treated as a survivor rather than being thought of as a victim, you must first stop being a victim. While working at a local domestic violence shelter I was always mystified when a woman came up missing and we later discovered that she had decided to return home to her abuser.

Police will tell you that about half of the domestic violence calls they respond to end with the victim defending the abuser to the police who have come to help her. In short, if someone is abusing you currently you must make it stop. If you can't find a way to make it end and preserve the relationship, then you must leave the relationship. Accept that these are your only choices. Continuing with an abusive relationship will only guarantee you a future filled with violence and pain. As the old saying states, "If you keep doing what you have always done you are sure to keep getting what you've always gotten."

Forgive Yourself

Set aside 30-60 minutes to think about your life as it regards to the traumas you have suffered, and your journey towards hearing. This will not be pleasant and you may be tempted to skip this activity, but if you are an adult woman you have most likely been traumatized by something or someone in the past. Even if the trauma was not severe enough to cause PTSD, it may still be causing residual effects in your life. Today is as good a time as any to confront it, get past it, and heal. Respond to the questions please.

Questions
Briefly describe the situation in which you were traumatized or victimized.
What aspect of the situation do you feel was your fault?
What did you learn from the situation?
Did anything good come from what you went through? If so, list those things.
What do you need to forgive yourself for?
How will you forgive yourself?
How will you know that you have been successful in moving past the negative space you occupied due to the trauma?
Is there anyone else you need to forgive? Anyone who disbelieved you or told you that you somehow deserved the violence you encountered and reinforced your sense of guilt or shame?
How will you let these people know that you forgive them?

Congratulations! You have looked at a painful period in your life and perhaps you have discovered some aspects of your situation that you have failed to consider in the past. Do you feel the light entering the wound? The light is insight, a new perspective on a past trauma. The light is strength born from the knowledge that you have survived what is likely the worst thing that will ever happen to you. You know now that it is true, what doesn't kill you makes you stronger. The light is returning you to being your true self, bloodied, but not bowed. The light is a renewed zest for life, and a determination to do great things despite of, or even because of, your own past suffering.

It was incredible to see the woman whose toddler died transform as she sat in my class after she spoke about her son's death and slowly to let go of her guilt. We could almost see it leave her body, as one by one every other woman in the room quietly walked to where she sat and hugged her. They told her the truth of her situation, that there was nothing she could have done short of never meeting the murdering boyfriend in the first place, that would have changed the outcome. By the time she the session ended she appeared transformed, and let it be known that she was "ready to begin living again" after 18 years of self-imposed isolation. She felt ready to connect with others again, to trust herself in her selection of friends, and to heal.

So what's wrong with her anyway?

When a woman is suffering the people around her scratch their heads and wonder why she continues to remain in a destructive relationship or situation. Some reasons that women stay in violent relationships are:

- An extremely dependent relationship
- False, illusionary feelings of control over the situation
- Ongoing hope for the relationship
- Traditional ideology/vows
- Emotional reactions (feeling of deserving)

To leave domestic violence, a woman needs:

- A place to live
- A source of income
- Child care arrangements
- Transportation

In most cases, battered women and children will remain at risk because:

- They believe they need the resources of person who is battering them
- They believe there will be no further acts of violence
- They are still in love with the abuser

In short, woman who stay believe they cannot survive without the abuser. And if a woman believes that she is probably right. Her mindset alone will keep her from breaking free of the situation. But she will feel like a fool for staying. I have heard hundreds of stories of abuse from women over the past decade, and when I ask them why they stayed, they respond overwhelmingly, "embarrassment." They don't admit the abuse to others, or seek help because they can't face the fact that they were fooled into trusting the abuser. Some women even go out of their way to cover up what is happening, and play it off to themselves and others as something that isn't as serious as it looks.

Yet others are awaiting rescue. They don't attempt to cover up the abuse, but allow themselves to be seen as pathetic and victimized, hoping that a friend or family member will swoop in and provide the means for them to

leave. This tactic leaves women feeling foolish too when the rescue never comes. The real key to escaping an abusive relationship is to first believe that you can get out, and then begin planning your own way out.
I know a woman who started planning her way out the first time her husband assaulted her. After two years of secretly saving money, learning to drive, and locating an affordable apartment in an acceptable school district she left one day while he was at work, with him being none the wiser of her plan. He came home to find divorce papers on the kitchen counter and an empty house. What strength and cunning it must have taken to prepare for her exit without a hint of her plans to anyone.

If you are struggling to leave an abusive relationship, know that you don't have to do it alone. Contact your local batter's women's shelter to learn what resources might be available. Tell someone you trust what is happening to you, and ask them to assist you in planning your exit. Pack a "go bag" in the event that you need to run before you are ready to leave. The bag should contain the following items:

- Money, at least $100 in case you need to rent a car or get a hotel room
- A credit card that is in your name alone
- An extra set of car keys
- Medications for yourself and your children—at least a three-day supply
- Legal papers—birth certificates, passports, shot records for the children, social security cards
- A disposable cell phone programmed with the numbers of your friends, relatives, police, and the nearest battered women's shelter
- Shoes and warm clothes in case you have to leave at night wearing pajamas.
- Snack food and bottled water in case you have to stay hidden for a long period

Hide the go bag somewhere where you will be able to retrieve it easily, and where he won't notice it. To avoid him tracking you after you leave home take the battery out of your phone as soon as you are a safe distance away and begin using your disposable phone instead.

Where there is a will there is a way, and you must find it if you are to transition from being a victim to being a survivor. The road is long and the way is perilous for victims of domestic violence. To keep yourself and your children safe from the abuser you may have to change your job, your children's school, your gym, grocery, and church, and stay away from the homes of your friends and relatives. You may even need to relocate to a different community, but it will be worth it. You will be safe, and you can begin to heal.

Wounds Both Big and Small

You may be feeling relieved right now that you have no deep wounds to heal if you are among the 40% of the population who has never suffered violence at the hands of another. But almost daily most women are assailed with a variety of small wounds, insults or disrespect. Hateful words from your children, an inattentive spouse, or a meddling, judgmental friend, coworker or relative may be the perpetrator of these hurts. None of us escape life without a few dings in our self-esteem and hurt feelings.

The best revenge is just moving on and getting over it. Don't give someone the satisfaction of watching you suffer

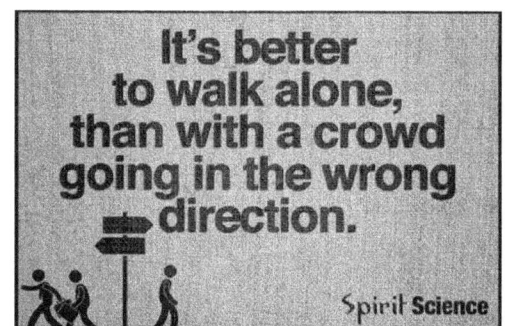

The trick is not to become a "wound collector." Joe Navarro, a former FBI agent turned author, coined this phrase to explain people who never move past the slights that we all experience from time to time. Wound Collectors not only accumulate and dwell on their own wounds, they also find others who have suffered similar wrongs and add those grievances to their own list as proof that there is something inherently wrong about the thing or person that hurt them. Collecting these wounds justifies them in striking back and retaliating against others. In the extreme, Would Collectors become a significant danger to others that they blame for their pain because as the wounds stack up the Collector feels justified in doing great harm in retaliation. For the wound collector, there is no fixing things, only the collection of slights.

To remain mentally healthy we must move past old hurts, let time heal the wounds, and actively work to leave our wounds in the rearview mirror. Sometimes that means assertively confronting the offender and asking for a better deal. This is where the assertive talking philosophies and negotiation skills learned in the last chapter will come in handy. But sometimes no amount of reason will change how the other person thinks, feels and behaves. It is then that you must take care of yourself by sending yourself sane and rational messages about the situation.

Remind yourself often that you are a lovable and capable person who treats others with integrity. Feel proud of yourself for not lowering yourself to the other person's level. Stop ruminating about the situation and channel your thoughts towards future possibilities instead of dwelling on past hurts. Put things in proper perspective. Use the time honored "Ann Landers" approach. Ask yourself whether you are better off with or without this person or situation in your life. Give it ample thought. If the answer is that you would be better off without the person who is wounding you, devise an exit plan.

This may mean that you will need to break off contact with this person or situation permanently. You should be absolutely sure that there is no chance for success in your current situation before you make a move, but once you decide to depart you need to do so in a decisive, organized manner if possible. It's usually not a good idea to end a relationship quickly however except in cases of abuse or other extreme conditions.

It's better to walk alone, than with a crowd going in the wrong direction.

Spirit Science

Remember the woman whose husband killed his mistress during their marriage? She revealed that he also physically abused her, but despite all of this she went to visit him weekly in jail during the five years that he was incarcerated for manslaughter. The day he was released from prison she presented him divorce papers.

When I asked why she didn't leave when her husband went to jail she said it was because she wanted to be absolutely sure that he couldn't be rehabilitated before breaking her wedding vows. If this woman is able to give her marriage a chance we should all probably work first to rehabilitate our relationships before giving up on them. It is difficult to leave someone or something that you love, but it is always better to leave and start anew than to continue to suffer ongoing wounds, whether big or small. People who wound you tend to rob you of your joy, and you cannot be a truly great woman if you aren't able to feel joyful about your life and your possibilities.

Should I stay or should I go now?

There are a myriad of reasons why people leave relationships, some due to significant relationship distress and others because they grow bored, or just don't feel fully committed to another person. Whatever your reasons for leaving, it is important to be certain in your own heart and mind that you are doing the right thing. Here are seven substantial reasons to consider giving another person their walking papers and continuing your life without them.

1.) **Physical abuse:** Never forgive a second incidence of physical abuse, and think long and hard about whether you should consider forgiveness after the first incidence. Physical abuse usually gets progressively worse over time, so if you notice a pattern of escalating abuse you need to plan your exit.

2.) **Addiction:** Consider leaving if gambling, drugs, alcohol or any other addictive behavior your partner has gets to the point that it becomes a problem and is affecting your wellbeing and your ability trust them. If they continue their addictive behavior despite promises to stop know that their primary love interest is now their addiction and not you.

3.) **Deception:** If you can't be yourself or you can't do things you want to do because it will hurt or anger the other person, maybe you should find someone else who will appreciate you for you or not be in a relationship at all. If you are being lied to or you are constantly lying to someone else to maintain peace, it's time to stop deceiving yourself and end your relationship. If you can't be honest with one another you cannot partner effectively together and you need either bring an end to the lying or go your separate ways.

4.) **Cheating:** Unless you have an agreement to be in an open relationship, cheating is unacceptable. It is possible to forgive someone for cheating and move on, usually if the situation was extremely complex and both parties contributed to it. Forgiveness may work only if both parties are willing to make the necessary changes and put the past behind them. It won't be easy but it is possible. However, if the person is a habitual cheater who just wants to have their cake and eat it too, regardless of your feelings, then it's time to leave while you can still respect yourself.

5.) **Disrespect:** This can come in many forms, but in this case I am referring to someone mistreating their partner through constant verbal abuse, mind games and degradation. If you're in a relationship where your partner is the type to put you down, talk down to you, and make a fool of you for the sake of laughter, then it's time to reconsider your relationship.

6.) **Lack of Balance:** If you are doing all of the giving, and the other person is doing all the taking, it is time to ask for a better deal. If the deal cannot be negotiated, or if the situation doesn't change, it will probably be easier to go it on your own rather than to drag the other person around with you like a ball and chain that is holding you back

7.) **Endless Drama:** If your relationship is a akin to a roller coaster ride it is time to decide if you need the ongoing highs and lows in your life. If your partner suffers endlessly over every slight, or keeps changing the rules of your relationship, it is time to re-evaluate your options. Unfortunately this sometimes occurs when your partner has a mental illness like bi-polar disorder, but even then you need to consider how much longer you want to play a supporting role in the soap opera that is their life.

Exit Plan

Take this brief assessment to help you think through a current situation where you are being hurt physically, emotionally or mentally. It may be a work situation, or one with a friend, relative, partner or acquaintance. After answering the questions posed you will be able to make a better informed decision about whether you need to cut your losses and leave, or hang in there and work out your differences.

If you decide to leave...
What resources will you need to put in place prior to leaving? How much money will you need to save up before departing? Where will you live or work after you leave?
Who can you count on for support during the exit process?
What will you do if the person begs you not to go or throws up obstacles to your departure?
How will you guarantee that you will not have contact with the person after you exit? What do you need to change so that they can't find you?
What are you willing to do if that person poses an ongoing threat to you after you leave?
What new activities will you begin pursuing soon after you leave to help you define and enjoy your new lifestyle?
How long will it take you to arrange your exit? What will you do between now and then to make sure that you are safe and that your life is bearable?

Create the life you would like for yourself moving forward. Everyone you meet has the potential to be a blessing or a lesson in your life. Use what you learned from this relationship to make the next one better.

A Real Woman

Lisa loathed Larry as much as she loved him. A "mean drunk," Larry would come home after a night of heavy drinking about once a month and awaken Lisa with his fists. He would pummel her back mostly so that the bruises weren't visible to her friends and coworkers. The next morning he is always pathetically sorry and vowed to stop drinking. He tried to make up for the bruises by being his sweetest self for the next few days. He cooked, cleaned, bought her gifts and wrote the most beautiful love notes that he could muster. He would even take her out for a night on the town and tell everyone they encountered how much he loved Lisa and what a wonderful person she was.

Lisa felt like such a fraud. Her friends and relatives all thought that Larry is a great guy and told Lisa how lucky she was to have found him. While Larry was showing her his good side Lisa was in full agreement. She would think back to when she fell in love with him, and the warm feelings of those early days came flooding back. Then he would fail to come home after work and she knew where he is, at the bar spending his entire paycheck on liquor and ladies.

Finally, bruised and in financial ruin, Lisa could no longer pretend that all was well. While attending a family reunion Lisa told her favorite cousin Fran of her dilemma. "How long have the two of you been together?" Fran inquired. "Five years," Lisa responded. "And did the hitting start shortly after you married? Fran asked. "Yes,"

Lisa replied, "I have all this time invested in this relationship, and I still love him...sometimes, but he refuses to go to counseling, and I don't see things getting any better unless he does."

"How old are you," Fran queried although she already knew the answer. "I am 32," Lisa answered. "So you have about 50 more years left to live," Fran calculated. "How many more years will you invest in Larry knowing that it is unlikely that he will stop abusing you?" Fran wondered aloud.

The question kept Lisa awake that night. More than anything Lisa wanted to be a mom, but bringing a child into their relationship was unthinkable, and her biological clock was ticking. Lisa suddenly realized that she would go from feeling like a fraud to feeling like a fool if she missed her chance to have a family of her own while waiting for Larry to grow up himself. "Wasting five years in a dead end relationship is long enough," Lisa thought. "Investing another five, ten or twenty years with him is too crazy to even consider."

The next day Lisa began to formulate her exit plan. She priced apartments, arranged to have their house appraised, and devised a budget to support herself until the house could be sold. Knowing that Larry would turn up at her job, her church and her spin class to beg her to return, Lisa began to search for a new job that would pay a bit more, and was conveniently located in proximity of the apartment complex where she planned to rent her new apartment. She found a church in the area as well, and was pleased to learn that there was an onsite gym in the complex where she could spin to her heart's content.

Six months after she made the decision to leave Lisa rented a moving van and with her cousin's help vacated her home while Larry was at work. She left divorce papers on the kitchen counter, with a note telling Larry goodbye, thanking him for the good times, and suggesting that he contact her attorney if he had questions.

Life was not easy for the remainder of the year. As predicted Larry begged and raged, and did everything he could to find her, but he didn't prevail. Lisa's life was lonely at first and she often felt as though there wasn't another person on the planet that cared about her as much as she had thought Larry did. But slowly, things began to turn around. Fran introduced Lisa to Monica, another woman who was recently divorced, and they started hanging out together. Monica was an artist and asked Lisa to come along and help her sell her art at fairs and festivals on weekends.

Nine months after her divorce Lisa met Matt, another artist who was selling his wares in the booth next to Monica's at the county fair. Lisa and Matt were married a year later. On their second wedding anniversary Lisa gave birth to their first child, a baby girl with curly dark hair and huge brown eyes.

Does Lisa still think about the time she spent with Larry? Hardly ever. She is much too busy living the life she always wanted. She no longer feels like a fraud or a fool, she feels lucky...fortunate that she is no longer with Larry, and grateful that she did not waste another day of her wonderful life waiting for a change in him that would never come.

Each One Teach One

"Never doubt that a small group of thoughtful, committed citizens can change the world: indeed it is the only thing that ever has." Margaret Mead

What fun would it be to become a greater woman if you have to leave the people you love behind to do it? It happens you know. You grow, and improve yourself and your place in the world, and the other people in your life remain as they have always been. This never bodes well for your relationship with them. You become bored, or they get jealous and you begin to see less and less of each other. You can always make new friends, or choose to see your relatives only on special occasions, or you can limit your conversations to superficial topics so as not to show off your new-found expertise.

How unsatisfying does that sound? Thankfully there is another alternative. You can raise others up with you as you are on the rise. Perhaps not everyone will want to join you on your journey to be a greater woman, but you may be pleasantly surprised by how many other woman that you know might want to improve themselves.

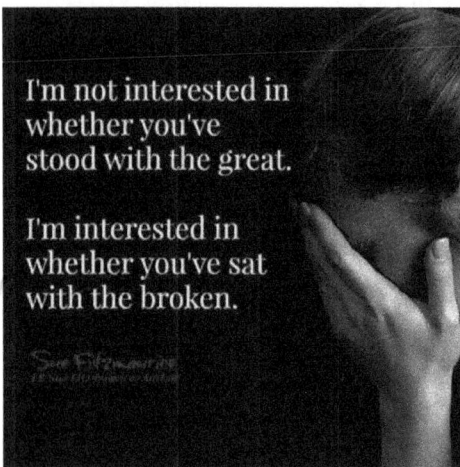

I'm not interested in whether you've stood with the great.

I'm interested in whether you've sat with the broken.

As you have worked your way through the introspective activities in this book you may have skipped a chapter or two, because you didn't have the time, or the interest in improving in a given area. Or you might feel you have already mastered some aspects of your personhood discussed herein, and you didn't feel you needed to do more work in those areas.

It will be the same with those you know. Some will want to join you in learning new things, but not others. I can always find a friend or two who wants to discuss how to make better food choices, but those same people are not at all interested in exercise options. Other friends are willing to join me in a thought-provoking discussion about spiritual development, but talking about finding a soulmate is something that they just don't believe is possible. Regardless, I try to help every woman I know learn the things she is interested in knowing, and value her for what she brings to my life.

Where Did Women's Liberation Go?

It was women that stopped the women's movement that began in 1960's America. By 1990 the women's liberation movement was no longer a force to be reckoned with. In fact, young women found the idea of being more liberated to be repugnant. Many blamed the women's libbers of the 1970's and 1980's for ruining their lives. They yearned to turn back the clock to the 1950's when women stayed home and men supported them financially. Yes, liberation brings not only benefits but increased responsibility as well.

According to 2013 study of women done by the Center for American Progress in 1969 only one-third of the American workforce was female. Now nearly half of all workers are women, but white women only make $.77 on the male dollar. It is much worse for women of color with African-American women earning $.64 and Hispanic women earning only $.54 on the white male dollar. Only one in ten mothers was the family's sole breadwinner in 1960, but in 2011 the number has risen to four in ten. Nationally, approximately 18% of women live below the poverty line. It seems like the more women work the further behind they fall.

Most women who work are not given paid family, medical or disability leave and 12.5% of women who work are uninsured when it comes to health insurance. On leadership, while 2012 saw more women than ever being elected to Congress, 15 states have no female elected leaders in the House of Representatives or the Senate. Congress remains 81.9% male. We have come a long way baby, but it seems we have a lot further to go if women ever hope to attain an equal share of the American dream.

Discrimination in any form is insulting, unfair and mean spirited, but discrimination against women is just plain stupid. Woman compose the MAJORITY of people on the planet. Now how can the minority (in the U.S. 50.8% of the population is female, 49.2 male) of the population hold down the majority? They are outnumbered! Do you think this means we are complicit in our own plight? I do. That is why I refuse to stop advocating for women. That is why I ask you to take up the fight with me.

Women stopped working for their own cause prematurely. We allowed our success to slow us down, then to stop us. As 1970's feminists we thought that if we simply put women's equality in motion that it would be carried forward by its own momentum. But that was not to be. Counter movements sprang up. "Total woman" ideology surfaced and advised women to play up their sexuality and manipulate their men into caring for them. Women were to be passive and allow men to control their lives and pay their way. The anti-choice movement was launched to counter the progress we had made towards giving a woman the right to control her own body with the Roe vs. Wade ruling. Workplace sexual harassment laws were disregarded with impunity, and women continued to be treated as second class citizens at work and at home.

The saddest part for me was that these counter causes were led by women. And they still are. The anti-Obamacare movement wants to end healthcare for "working poor" women in the U.S. and yet, the charge is being led by conservative women. The never-ending struggle to overturn Roe vs. Wade is led by women. And women always seem to be the first to ask what she did to deserve it when another woman is raped or beaten. The effort to defeat a raise in the national minimum wage, a move that would greatly help women and families, is being put forth by women who are afraid that they will have to pay more for their goods and services if the employees who work in the establishments that serve them were to be paid a living wage!

Good Help is Hard to Find

"What can I do?" you might ask. Well, let's start by talking about how to provide meaningful help to other women in order to form a powerful coalition of women that can carry our cause forward. Not one of you has gotten where you are without the help of another woman. In the space below list five women who have helped you the most since your arrival on the planet. Next to each name say how they helped you or what you learned from them.

Who helped you?	How were you helped?	What did you learn?
1.		
2.		
3.		
4.		
5.		

I am willing to bet that most of you named your mother and/or your grandmother, or another close female relative who guided you when you were a child and provided support, encouragement and assistance to you well into womanhood. Then there is probably a friend or two on your list, and perhaps a work mentor as well.

The purpose of this activity is twofold. First, it is beneficial to reflect on how your life has been enriched by other women. Where would you be now without their assistance? This might be a good time to contact these women and let them know why you are better for having known them. Women are shown so little appreciation, and now is the time to appreciate a woman who has helped you.

The second purpose of this exercise is to help you identify ways to pay the help you received forward. Do you know a woman right now that needs the same sort of help that you received from other women as you grew into your own? If so, it is time to make another call. Offer your help to the woman in need without judgment or reservation. Help her willingly and joyfully. This is an opportunity to pass along your legacy to someone who will one day pass it along to someone else. In this way your spirit and your essence will remain long after you have departed this earthly existence.

Now here is the rub. Not every woman you offer to help will want your assistance. Some won't be ready to hear what you have to say. Others might feel offended or criticized by your offer. Still others may be disinterested, or feel that they are not in need of any help. You must word your offer of assistance carefully in order to avoid misunderstanding. Below is a script that you can use to state your intentions in the most constructive and positive manner possible.

(Woman's name) _____, I am contacting you because I have noticed that you are wrestling with an issue about _____. I have had some experience with that issue myself and would be willing to lend you a helping hand or a listening ear. What is bothering you most about your current situation?

Notice that there is no unsolicited advice attached to your offer. How often in your life have you actually accepted and used unsolicited advice from someone else regardless of the quality of the suggestion? We tend to "yes but…", and "what if…" advice from others. We seldom feel that they have a good enough understanding of our situation to come up with the perfect solution for us. The advice that we tend to accept is solicited advice, the advice we ask for.

Advice often isn't the sort of help that we need as women. Someone who will simply listen empathetically is a real gift in a time of trouble. Women are wired to feel better as they talk through their issues. The sound of their own voice exploring the dimensions of their issues aloud is often enough to help them generate ideas as to how they can assist themselves in a sticky situation.

Judgment and condemnation is even less appreciated than unsolicited advice. Having another woman tell you what is wrong with you is humiliating and anger producing. Isn't it enough that the woman is in a tight spot without another member of the sisterhood letting her know that she got herself into the jam she is in? She probably already knows that if that is the case.

Here are five magic questions that you can ask another, or yourself, to help think through a difficult issue. Think of a situation that you are facing currently and answer these questions for yourself so you will know the benefit to be derived from this guided inquiry.

1. Given the situation you are in what would you like to as a result?
2. What are three options available to you to get the result you want?
3. What are the risks attached to each option? (What might go wrong with each option?)
4. Which set of risks is most under your control, and what will you do to keep the risks from occurring?
5. What is your plan?

Another way to help other women is to inspire them. You can do this by setting a great example, being open and honest about your own experiences, and providing encouragement. Recently I have been struggling with a number of issues related to family and business. I confided in a friend that I was feeling fatigued by the ongoing dramas and that I didn't know how much longer I could fight the good fight. Within a few minutes I received an email with "Hope this helps!" written in the subject line. The poem *Carry On* by Robert William Service appeared in the body of the email. She had tailored it to reflect female references as opposed to male pronouns in the original poem.

Carry On

It's easy to fight when everything's right,
And you're mad with the thrill and the glory;
It's easy to cheer when victory's near,
And wallow in fields that are gory.
It's a different song when everything's wrong,
When you're feeling infernally mortal;
When it's ten against one, and hope there is none,
Buck up, little soldier girl, and chortle:

Carry on! Carry on!
There isn't much punch in your blow.
You're glaring and staring and hitting out blind;
You're muddy and bloody, but never you mind.
Carry on! Carry on!
You haven't the ghost of a show.
It's looking like death, but while you've a breath,
Carry on, my daughter! Carry on!

And so in the strife of the battle of life
It's easy to fight when you're winning;
It's easy to slave, and starve and be brave,
When the dawn of success is beginning.
But the woman who can meet despair and defeat
With a cheer, there's the woman of God's choosing;
The woman who can fight to Heaven's own height
Is the woman who can fight when she's losing.

Carry on! Carry on!
Things never were looming so black.
But show that you haven't a cowardly streak,
And though you're unlucky you never are weak.
Carry on! Carry on!
Brace up for another attack.
It's looking like hell, but -- you never can tell:
Carry on, old girl! Carry on!

There are some who drift out in the deserts of doubt,
And some who in brutishness wallow;
There are others, I know, who in piety go
Because of a Heaven to follow.
But to labor with zest, and to give of your best,
For the sweetness and joy of the giving;
To help folks along with a hand and a song;
Why, there's the real sunshine of living.

Carry on! Carry on!
Fight the good fight and true;
Believe in your mission, greet life with a cheer;
There's big work to do, and that's why you are here.
Carry on! Carry on!
Let the world be the better for you;
And at last when you die, let this be your cry:
Carry on, my soul! Carry on!

I needed to be reminded that it was easy to be strong when there is little need for strength, and this poem hit the mark. I so love my friends. They always seem to know what I need and just how to give it to me so I will accept their gift of caring and love.

All Lives Matter

As this *work on you* book draws to an end, I hope you feel greater...stronger, more confident, self-esteeming and proud. I want you to be pleased with your progress, impressed with results, and delighted with the enriched life you are cultivating for yourself. You matter...whether you are young or old, female or male, brown, white, black, red or yellow...you matter. And you can change the world. You have already begun by changing yourself.

My final wish for you is that you be happy. Find a little time each day to do something for yourself or someone else that creates happiness. If you inspire happiness in others you will simultaneously bring it out in yourself.

Remember, no one has the power to make you happy except you. Others may try with flowers, candy, apologies, or jokes, but only you can decide whether to accept or reject their gifts of happiness. Whenever possible choose to be happy.

My husband recently did something that made me very happy. He is such a loving man! He proofread this book for me because he is much better at finding my errors than I am! Upon completing his editing duties he revealed that he felt so inspired by the book that he wanted to write a song in keeping with its theme. Here are Lou's lyrics, along with our best hopes that you become all you were meant to be.

Greater Woman in a Lesser World

Once I was a little girl,
Piggy tails and curly curls,
Now I'm no longer a little girl...
Greater woman in a lesser world.

Sitting at my mama and my daddy's knee,
As they taught me who I had to be,
When I grew up I could see,
It was me who had to find me.

You can be anything that you want to be,
You can be anything that you dream,
You can be anything you want to be,
She thought she could so she did!

Many challenges along the way,
Overcoming obstacles every day,
There is one thing I can say,
It made me who I am today.

Now I've finally found the key,
Gotta be the best that I can be,
I'm no longer that little girl,
Greater woman in a lesser world...

Join our facebook group at https://www.facebook.com/groups/greaterwomaninalesserworld/
Email Rita at ritar@rizzoandassociates.com
Visit our website at www.rizzoandassociates.com

78

www.ingramcontent.com/pod-product-compliance
Lightning Source LLC
Chambersburg PA
CBHW081520040426

42447CB00013B/3282